Landmark Speeches

OF NATIONAL SOCIALISM

MW01258486

LANDMARK SPEECHES
A Book Series

Martin J. Medhurst, General Editor

LANDMARK SPEECHES

OF

NATIONAL

SOCIALISM

Edited and with Translations by
Randall L. Bytwerk

TEXAS A&M UNIVERSITY PRESS   COLLEGE STATION

LIBRARY OF CONGRESS CATALOGING-IN-PUBLICATION DATA

Landmark speeches of National Socialism / [compiled and introduced by]
Randall L. Bytwerk. — 1st ed.
     p. cm. — (Landmark speeches, a book series)
    Includes index.
    ISBN-13: 978-1-60344-014-1 (cloth : alk. paper)
    ISBN-10: 1-60344-014-3 (cloth : alk. paper)
    ISBN-13: 978-1-60344-015-8 (pbk. : alk. paper)
    ISBN-10: 1-60344-015-1 (pbk. : alk. paper)
    1. Nazi propaganda.   2. Speeches, addresses, etc., German.
3. Nationalsozialistische Deutsche Arbeiter-Partei—History—Sources.
4. National socialism—History—Sources.
5. Germany—History—1933–1945—Sources.   I. Bytwerk, Randall L.
DD253.L298   2008
324.243'0238—dc22   2007037687

Für Dr. Robert D. Brooks,

einen Mann ohne Beispiel

CONTENTS

Landmark Speeches

OF NATIONAL SOCIALISM

The Magic Force of the Spoken Word

The National Socialist Approach to Rhetoric

National Socialism was the most prolific rhetorical movement of the twentieth century.[1] It depended on public speaking both from necessity (particularly in its early years) and principle. Hitler expressed the party's fundamental focus on public speaking in his semi-autobiographical book *Mein Kampf*, published in 1925: "[T]he power which has always started the greatest religious and political avalanches in history rolling has from time immemorial been the magic power of the spoken word, and that alone."[2] After the Nazis took power, a propagandist wrote: "When coming generations look back on the period of struggle and development of the National Socialist movement, one of the most interesting and significant conclusions they will draw is that seldom in the history of the German people,[3] indeed that of humanity itself, did the spoken word, that direct personal contact between the leader of a young and rising movement and the whole people, have such importance as in this significant period in the history of the German people."[4]

The speeches in this book provide a representative sample of the rhetoric that moved a civilized nation to support Nazism, and to close its eyes to the crimes that were not difficult to see. After 1945, many Germans claimed that they had not known what was happening—but that is not persuasive. Nazism was vague in the details of its plans, but clear as to its goals. Everything that Nazism intended was revealed in its rhetoric. He who had ears could have heard.

Hitler claimed no originality on propaganda, writing that he had learned its principles by studying the Church, the Marxist parties, and Germany's enemies. Propaganda, he argued, is an art, the basic principles of which might be learned by anyone, but mastery depended on innate ability.

He thought that the average person is uninterested in complex arguments, being ruled more by emotion than intellect. Nazi rhetoric therefore avoided presenting detailed solutions to complex problems. The effective leader, Hitler thought, made things seem simple, and could "make even adversaries far removed from one another seem to belong to a single category."[5] A speaker who attempts to persuade an audience by a complicated, developed argument, or by attacking multiple enemies, is doomed to fail.

A speaker should aim at the lowest common denominator, speaking so that everyone in the audience could understand. "[A]mong a thousand speakers there is perhaps only a single one who can manage to speak to locksmiths and university professors at the same time, in a form which not only is suitable to the receptivity of both parties, but also influences both parties with equal effect or actually lashes them into a wild storm of applause."[6] Hitler was confident of his own ability to do that.

Propaganda also needed to be one-sided. Since the masses did not understand complex issues, presenting balanced arguments would only shake their confidence in the rightness of a cause. Hitler used propaganda during World War I as an example. The Germans, cursed by hyper-objectivity, he claimed, allowed public discussion about the degree of Germany's responsibility for the war, whereas the Allies, despite their protestations of free speech, accused Germany of being guilty, and sealed their argument with the Treaty of Versailles, which declared Germany entirely responsible for the war.

What propaganda does say needs to be repeated over and over again "until the last member of the public understands what you want him to understand by your slogan."[7] Only when an audience has heard a point made repeatedly will it begin to respond. Hitler did not mean that the message should be repeated in the same way, but rather that varied forms needed to be found to hammer an idea into an audience.

A speaker's physical presence makes oral rhetoric more flexible. A printed page is a finished product, Hitler wrote, unable to change its form from one reader to another, but a speech can be altered even as it is being given: "While the speaker gets a continuous correction of his speech from the crowd he is addressing, since he can always see in the faces of his listeners to what extent they can follow his arguments with understanding and whether the impression and the effects of his words lead to the desired goal—the writer does not know his readers at all."[8] A speech, then, even with the same basic content, can vary significantly as it is given to varied audiences.

A speaker, Hitler thought, should stand before an audience with the fervor of an evangelist preaching a religious faith. Passion, not rational argument, is the key to persuasion: " . . . all great movements are popular movements, volcanic eruptions of human passions and emotional sentiments, stirred either by the cruel Goddess of Distress or by the firebrand of the word hurled among the masses."[9] And the speaker's own passion is increased as he faces a responsive audience.

Hitler viewed the crowd as a powerful persuasive force. He described a person who "steps for the first time into a mass meeting and has thousands and thousands of people of the same opinions around him, when, as a seeker, he is swept away by three or four thousand others into the mighty effect of suggestive intoxication and enthusiasm, when the visible success and agreement of thousands confirm to him the rightness of the new doctrine and for the first time arouse doubt in the truth of his previous conviction—then he himself has succumbed to the magic influence of what we might designate as 'mass suggestion.'"[10] This is unlikely to happen to someone reading a book at home.

. Hitler's rhetorical views also reflected his "leadership principle." Leaders emerged through struggle, through reaching the masses, not through discussions around a conference table. Without direct, personal contact between a leader and his followers, a leader can never demonstrate his abilities. As Hitler wrote, "to be a leader means to be able to move the masses."[11] Think of the great leaders of history, he asked. The French Revolution spread not through books, but through fiery oratory. Marxism triumphed not because of Marx's thick books, but because of "tens of thousands of untiring agitators, from the great agitator down to the small trade-union official and the shop steward and discussion speaker; this work consisted of the hundreds of thousands of meetings at which, standing on the table in smoky taverns, these people's orators hammered at the masses and thus were able to acquire a marvelous knowledge of this human material which really put them in a position to choose the best weapons for attacking the fortress of public opinion."[12] A public speech provided the opportunity for a politician to demonstrate his ability to lead. If he failed to win an audience, he failed the test of leadership.

To understand Nazi propaganda, whether in 1930 or today, one turns to Adolf Hitler. Other Nazis had important roles in propaganda, but no one had nearly as central a role in determining its nature and basic principles. Goebbels was a master of the tactics of propaganda, and had a central role in building the vast Nazi propaganda system, but even he reflected Hitler's thinking on broad issues.

In sum, Nazism saw oratory as an indispensable method of propaganda, the best way to reach the masses. Without it, they said, they could neither have won power in the first place, nor held on to it afterwards.

Early Nazi Speaking

Hitler joined the insignificant group in Munich that became the National Socialist German Workers Party in 1919. In his flattering account of the party's growth, he explained how he worked to persuade the other members to hold public meetings at which he soon became the primary speaker. He described his first public speech: "I spoke for thirty minutes, and what before I had simply felt within me, without in any way knowing it, was now proved by reality: I could speak! After thirty minutes the people in the small room were electrified. . . ."[13] By the end of 1920, he had spoken to over thirty mass meetings (with audiences ranging from 800 to 2,500), and in February 1921, he drew over 6,000.[14] Most were in Munich, but he began to speak elsewhere, too.

He remained the party's leading speaker during the years 1920–1933, when the Nazis were fighting to gain political power. The party went dormant when Hitler was in prison, and its growth suffered significantly when most German states banned his public speeches from 1926 to 1928 (he was allowed to speak to closed party meetings). The dearest hope of every Nazi group in Germany was to secure Hitler as a speaker. A large attendance was certain, and the admission fees Nazis charged for their meetings were welcome to party units that were always under financial stress. During the final election campaigns leading up to the Nazi takeover, Hitler spoke regularly to mass meetings of tens of thousands. He became the political rock star of Germany after 1930, drawing huge crowds to spectacular mass meetings. In a campaign innovation, he flew to as many as five cities on the same day, speaking to audiences that sometimes exceeded 100,000.[15]

His persuasive speaking, and the effect of being part of a huge crowd, transformed many Germans who attended his meetings. Goebbels, addressing party propagandists in 1928, said: "I have met people who had attended a Hitler meeting for the first time, and at the end they said: 'This man put in words everything I have been searching for for years. For the first time, someone gave expression to what I want.'"[16] Goebbels is hardly unbiased, but numerous contemporary accounts testify to Hitler's ability to captivate large audiences.

Hitler was not the only top Nazi speaker. Goebbels, Hermann Göring, Julius Streicher, Gregor Strasser, and others, also attracted large audiences. The Nazis developed a cadre of speakers qualified to speak to audiences of varying types. Some were licensed to speak to the entire country. Others could speak only at meetings in their area. The party even developed a correspondence course that trained about six thousand speakers before 1933.[17]

Nazi meetings were more than gatherings at which someone gave a speech. In the early days of movies and radio, and before television, political meetings were a form of entertainment. Whenever possible, the Nazis turned their meetings into events. There were bands, marching, flags and banners, the thrill of being part of a crowd. The speech remained the center, but the Nazis realized that, if people were to return to their meetings time after time to hear basically the same message, meetings had to hold their interest.[18]

The result was an unprecedented campaign of political meetings. The party claimed to have organized 34,000 meetings before the *Reichstag* election in September 1930 and 50,000 within two weeks of the 13 March 1932 presidential elections.[19] In some areas, the Nazis held more political meetings than all other political parties combined (there were as many as thirty other parties). In 1932, after the Nazi Party had become the largest German political party, Goebbels wrote: "The National Socialist movement grew not because of its journalists, but because of its speakers."[20] He was correct.

RHETORIC IN THE THIRD REICH

When Hitler took power in 1933, some expected the rhetorical flood to end, but the Nazis thought differently. As the party magazine for propagandists put it in 1937:

> Now and again, one still encounters the completely wrong idea that since National Socialism has taken power, meetings and speeches no longer have the same significance as they did when we were fighting for power. He who wants to reduce the number of meetings, or take less care in holding them, thereby proves that he has never understood the nature of the National Socialist movement. Just as a religion or a church can never stop preaching and explaining the faith in a thousand ways from the pulpit, no more can National Socialism surrender the direct and powerful effect of the speech, which ever and again strengthens the faith of the movement and provides new power for the never-ending struggle.[21]

With power came even more rhetoric, because the Nazis knew that coercion was not enough to maintain power—people had to be persuaded, even in a dictatorship. Hitler had written in *Mein Kampf*: "A movement with great aims must therefore be anxiously on its guard not to lose contact with the broad masses."[22] Force was an important form of propaganda—but the Nazis were convinced that, as Goebbels wrote, sitting on bayonets is uncomfortable.[23] To maintain power required unceasing efforts to persuade Germans that National Socialism deserved their unconditional allegiance.

Before 1933, Hitler drew large audiences, but his speeches were rarely broadcast over the radio, and then only in part, nor did non-party newspapers carry his speeches. After 1933, his speeches became major events. They were broadcast in full over national radio, printed in every newspaper, shown in part in weekly newsreels, and reprinted in huge editions in books and pamphlets. Restaurants and pubs were expected to turn their radios on when Hitler spoke, and some cities erected public loudspeakers. Key passages from his speeches appeared in weekly posters with inspiring quotations, which were hung throughout Germany by the hundreds of thousands.[24]

The extensive Nazi propaganda system mobilized whenever Hitler spoke. His speeches were major events, as instructions to local propagandists in 1939 demonstrated:

> The Führer's words are seeds in the people's hearts. . . . The task of each propagandist, therefore, is to guard the national experience of each Führer speech, to nourish the flame of enthusiasm, ever to encourage it. He will be able to do this if he gives his full devotion and earnestness to studying each word, letting them work on him each day anew. Then his conversations with citizens will be imbued with a glimmer of the rousing and unifying power that dwells in all the Führer's words.[25]

And there is no doubt that Germans attended to Hitler's words. The Nazi party and state carefully watched public sentiments. They noted the attentiveness with which Germans attended to Hitler's speeches, sometimes discussing them at length, despite the fact that he often spoke for two hours or more.

The standard edition of Hitler's speeches for 1932–1945 runs over three thousand pages in four volumes.[26] That is after the editor removed the sections in many speeches that recited the party's history. He spoke on major national holidays. At the Nuremberg rallies, held annually from 1933 to 1938, he spoke several times a day for over a week. He would speak to the youth, women, various party organizations, and so forth. And he spoke when events dictated (e.g., referendum campaigns, the beginning of World War II, after significant battles). Like his counterpart in England, Winston Churchill, Hitler did not depend on speechwriters. His style was inimitable, and every word was his.

Hitler was the most prominent orator of the Third Reich, but he had company. Nazi leaders spoke regularly to audiences throughout Germany. In the United States, even most presidential speeches are only printed in part by the average newspaper. One would not expect to see the texts of speeches by the vice president or the secretary of state regularly carried by every newspaper. In Germany, newspapers were filled with the full texts of lengthy speeches. Speeches by Goebbels, Hermann Göring, Rudolf Heß, Alfred Rosenberg, and other leaders were published in newspapers and reprinted in books and pamphlets with large editions.

And there was more. Beside the Nuremberg rally, Nazi regional and county organizations usually held annual rallies, filled with marching and speaking. The party speaker system expanded greatly after 1933. Thousands of speakers were licensed to speak to audiences of various sizes. Party subsidiaries such as the Hitler Youth and the National Socialist Women's League had their own corps of speakers. The tens of thousands of party leaders (extending down to the block level) often gave speeches on holidays and at public meetings, or to commemorate those who died in the war. Although the party told propagandists that citizens should not be ordered to attend meetings, poor attendance looked bad to superiors, and many party leaders used all the pressure they could to encourage people to come. The party's system of neighborhood block wardens went door to door to sell tickets to Nazi meetings. The party organized saturation campaigns, during which dozens, or even hundreds, of meetings were held in a city or region within a few days or weeks.

Statistics demonstrate the range of Nazi rhetorical activity. During May and June 1940, the party organization in Eastern Prussia held over three hundred meetings.[27] The whole party propaganda apparatus claimed to have held 200,000 meetings during the first fifteen months of the war.[28] During the period from October 1943 through April 1944, with the war situation critical and with 3,500 party speakers serving in the military, the Nazi party still organized nearly 71,000 meetings throughout the country.[29] Public meetings were part of life in the Third Reich.

Main Themes in Nazi Rhetoric

What was the content of the vast flow of Nazi rhetoric? Following Hitler's approach, it was simple, emotional, and repetitious, as the cross section of Nazi speeches in this book demonstrates. It includes three speeches by Adolf Hitler. The first was given when the Nazi Party was refounded in 1925, the second at the height of his military success in 1941, and third, his final delivered speech in January 1945. It includes four speeches by Joseph Goebbels, a campaign speech from 1932, a speech on propaganda at the 1934 Nuremberg Rally, one of his annual speeches on Hitler's birthday, and his most famous speech, the "Total War" speech from February 1943. There are speeches by Gerhard Wagner, a party racial expert, Gertrud Scholtz-Klink, the women's leader, and Julius Streicher, the most prominent anti-Semite. Finally, there are three model speeches intended to guide tens of thousands of local party leaders.

Every speech proclaims Hitler's greatness, in ways that become more inflated with time. Hitler himself is hardly modest. In 1925, he demands absolute, unquestioning obedience from his followers, though he admits to having made mistakes. At the height of his success in 1941, he presents himself as a far-seeing leader prepared for any eventuality. And even in his last public speech in 1945, he claims always to have been in the right, and is confident that Providence will lead him to victory, as it always had in the past. Goebbels argues that Hitler is the only person who can save Germany in 1932. He makes the same claim in his 1943 "Total War" speech, under dramatically different conditions. And in his 1937 speech on Hitler's birthday, he describes Hitler as a genius who understands every aspect of human life to the finest detail.

The other speeches reinforce the message. Gerhard Wagner thanks Hitler for his brilliant racial measures. Gertrud Scholtz-Klink asserts that German women owe everything to Hitler. Julius Streicher tells his audience that Hitler will bring them prosperity and solve the Jewish Question. And even at the end of the war,

German young people were promised that in swearing an oath to Hitler, they were guaranteeing their happy future. And this is only a small sampling of speeches building the Hitler myth, speeches reinforced by films like Leni Riefenstahl's *Triumph of the Will,* books, radio broadcasts, schools, and more. As the Nazi slogan had it, "The Führer is always right," a phrase hammered into German minds over the twelve years of Hitler's Reich.

Nazi rhetoric also proclaimed a worldview of religious reach.[30] As Kenneth Burke wrote in a still valuable essay in 1939: "Hitler appeals by relying upon a bastardization of fundamentally religious patterns of thought."[31] The party claimed to provide a full explanation of the universe, and guidance for everyday life. Hitler had written that "a man does not die for business, but only for ideals."[32] The Nazis drew upon existing German values, incorporating as their own great figures of German history such as Bismarck and Frederick the Great. They claimed to support a "positive Christianity" that transcended differences between Protestants and Catholics. Germans did not support Hitler because they expected him to lead them into ruinous war, but rather because he and his party drew upon deeply rooted values and beliefs.

The Nazi worldview is repeatedly addressed in the speeches in this book. In 1925, Hitler spoke of the movement's ideas, which he claimed "were ethical, immortal, imperishable, able to enlighten people in distant centuries." Scholtz-Klink spoke of "the great thought and the compelling idea of the people's community." Wagner outlined the racial side of the Nazi worldview, claiming that Nazism was following nature's own laws in eliminating "life unworthy of life." After Stalingrad, Goebbels argued that Germany was fighting for European values against Asiatic Bolshevism. And at the end of the war, Hitler claimed to be doing God's work in defending the German people. Throughout its history, Nazism presented itself not as a political party, but as a movement that encompassed everything Germans held to be true and just.

Anti-Semitism was at the core of the Nazi worldview, and nearly every speech in this collection attacks the Jews at some point. Hitler claims that Jews were responsible for Germany's problems before he took power, and in 1945 argues that he is fighting the culminating battle against the Jewish world enemy. Goebbels attacks the

Jews in three of the four speeches included here, neglecting them only in his encomium on Hitler.[33] Scholtz-Klink focuses on other matters, but notes in passing that German children learned more about Jewish history than their own, something she thinks should be remedied. Wagner focuses more on Nazi plans to improve the quality of the German race, but also mentions the Jews. Streicher rejects any pity for the Jews, and hopes that they will one day "receive the death penalty they deserve."

The trajectory of Nazism is also clear. In 1925, Hitler's movement was insignificant, but he prophesied Nazism's triumph. Up through 1942, Nazi rhetoric was triumphant, able to claim success after success. With Goebbels's "Total War" speech, the tone changes. Goebbels presented a grim military situation. Although he expressed confidence that Germany would win, he also made it clear that the consequences of losing the war would be terrible. The sample speeches from 1944 and 1945 reminded audiences of Nazism's achievements, but also stressed that the war was a matter of life or death, that Germany's very existence was at stake. Hitler stresses the same danger in his final speech.

What propaganda avoids saying is at least as important as what it does say. The Nazis realized that blatant lying often fails, and that people accept some things in general that they reject if they know the details. In his 1934 speech in Nuremberg, Goebbels praised the "truthfulness" of Nazi propaganda, and in practice he usually avoided outright lies. Two half-truths do not a full truth make, however. In reading these speeches, it is critical to "read between the lines," to look for what is omitted, for what is implicit but not clearly stated. For example, a logical conclusion of Wagner's discussion of "life unworthy of life" is that such life should be ended, something the Nazis did in private without discussing in public.

Rhetoric has consequences. The speeches in this book captivated many Germans, making, to quote Plato, the worse appear the better cause. In 1947, a poll found that 55 percent of Germans thought that National Socialism had been a good idea, but one badly carried out.[34] In 1951, 40 percent saw 1933–1938 as the best period in twentieth-century German history. Even after the war, Nazism's rhetoric was stronger in many people's minds than its reality.

The Germans who cheered Hitler, or Goebbels, or any of the multitude of other Nazi speakers, remind us of rhetoric's power to promote evil as well as good.

NOTES

1. The full name of the party was the National Socialist German Workers Party, a rhetorical construction that encompassed almost everything. The party preferred to speak of itself as "National Socialist." The word "Nazi" was used only rarely within the party, although it is the most common term in English.

2. Adolf Hitler, *Mein Kampf,* trans. Ralph Manheim (Boston: Houghton Mifflin, 1971), 106–107.

3. I consistently translate the German word *Volk* as "people." It is singular in German, but that reads awkwardly in English. By the word, the Nazis meant the totality of ethnic Germans conscious in some way of belonging to the "German race."

4. A. E. Frauenfeld, "Die Macht der Rede," *Unser Wille und Weg,* August 1937, 16. The article is available on the German Propaganda Archive, http://www.calvin.edu/cas/gpa/machtrede.htm. Future references to the site will take this form: GPA/machtrede.htm.

5. Hitler, 118.

6. Hitler, 342.

7. Hitler, 180–81.

8. Hitler, 469.

9. Hitler, 107.

10. Hitler, 478–79.

11. Hitler, 580.

12. Hitler, 472–73.

13. Hitler, 355.

14. Ian Kershaw, *Hitler 1889–1936: Hubris* (New York: W. W. Norton, 1998), 149.

15. See, for example, Heinrich Hoffmann and Josef Berchtold, *Hitler über Deutschland* (Munich: Franz Eher, 1932). Parts of the book are available on the GPA/hitler3.htm.

16. Joseph Goebbels, "Erkenntnis und Propaganda," *Signale der neuen Zeit. 25 ausgewählte Reden von Dr. Joseph Goebbels* (Munich: Franz Eher, 1934), 28–52. A full translation is available on the GPA/goeb54.htm.

17. For more information on early Nazi speaker training, see Randall L. Bytwerk, "Fritz Reinhardt and the *Rednerschule der NSDAP,*" *Quarterly Journal of Speech* 67 (1981), 298–309.

18. For more on the Nazi meeting system during the period, see Randall L. Bytwerk, "Rhetorical Aspects of the Nazi Meeting: 1926–1933," *Quarterly Journal of Speech* 61 (1975), 307–18.

19. *Völkischer Beobachter*, 17–18 August 1930, 13–14 March 1932. This was the party's daily newspaper.

20. Joseph Goebbels, *Kampf um Berlin. Der Anfang* (Munich: Franz Eher, 1934), 18.

21. Frauenfeld, 21.

22. Hitler, 107.

23. Joseph Goebbels, "Goldene Worte für einen Diktator und für solche, die es werden wollen," *Wetterleuchten. Aufsätze aus der Kampfzeit* (Munich: Franz Eher, 1939), 325–27. The article is translated in the GPA/angrif13.htm.

24. For examples, see GPA/wochenspruch.htm.

25. The full text is translated in the GPA/heimat.htm.

26. Max Domarus, *Hitler: Speeches and Proclamations 1932–1945*, 4 vols., trans. Mary Fran Gilbert (Waconda, IL: Bolchazy-Carducci, 1990–2004).

27. Bundesarchiv Berlin, NS 18/996, Gaupropagandaleitung Ostpreußen, "Bericht für die Monate Mai und Juni 1940."

28. "Die Arbeit der Partei-Propaganda im Kriege," *Unser Wille und Weg* 11 (1941), p. 1. A translation is available in the GPA/warprop.htm.

29. "Die Versammlungen der NSDAP. Eine Uebersicht über das Winterhalbjahr 1943/44," *Die Lage*, Folge 116B, June 1944. This was a publication for party officials.

30. For a more developed argument on Nazism as a worldview, see Randall L. Bytwerk, *Bending Spines: The Propagandas of Nazi Germany and the German Democratic Republic* (East Lansing, MI: Michigan State University Press, 2004).

31. "The Rhetoric of Hitler's Battle," reprinted in *The Philosophy of Literary Form* (New York: Vintage, 1957), 164–69.

32. Hitler, 152.

33. Only the first (1933) and last (1945) of the twelve speeches Goebbels delivered on Hitler's birthday mention the Jews at all. In 1933, there is a brief mention of the "Jewish-Marxist" police. In 1945, there are three references to an alleged international Jewish conspiracy directed against Germany. These speeches focused on building the myth of Hitler as leader.

34. Cited by Otto Dov Kolka, "The German Population and the Jews: State of Research and New Perspectives," in *Probing the Depths of German Antisemitism: German Society and the Jews, 1933–1941*, ed. David Bankier (New York: Berghahn Books, 2000), 279–80.

Adolf Hitler

Reestablishing the National Socialist German Workers Party

27 February 1925

Hitler joined the tiny German Workers Party in 1919. He quickly became its leader. On 9 November 1923, at the height of the great German inflation (on 20 November, one U.S. dollar was equal to four trillion German marks), Hitler risked a coup. He led his followers through the streets of Munich to the Feldherrnhalle, a war memorial, where waiting police opened fire. Sixteen of Hitler's followers were killed; Hitler himself was arrested, and after a trial that he turned into a political platform, he was sentenced to four years in prison. The party was banned, and its remnants degenerated into squabbling factions. Hitler stood outside the fray, using his time in prison to write *Mein Kampf*.

He was released in December 1924 after serving only nine months of his term, and set about rebuilding the party. The authorities lifted the ban on the Nazi Party on 16 February 1925. Hitler now arranged one of his rhetorical masterpieces: a mass meeting on 27 February to reestablish the party. He chose the same beer hall from which he had launched his abortive revolution fifteen months earlier. Three thousand people packed the hall, and several thousand more were turned away.

He entered to the passionate applause of the audience, and gave the two-hour speech that follows. Its first three-quarters offered nothing that most in the audience had not already heard, and would hear again in Hitler's future speeches. He reviewed

Germany's history, claiming that past conservative parties had no contact with the masses, and that leftist parties pretended to address the problems faced by ordinary Germans, but actually served the interests of the Jews who controlled them. He also outlined his views on propaganda.

In the last quarter of the speech, he moved to reestablish his control of the party. He claimed absolute authority. Anyone unwilling to obey could go his own way. Hitler "forgave" those who had made mistakes in his absence, and demanded that there be no criticism of him or the party for a year. The audience responded with enthusiasm.

After the speech, Hitler had arranged what Ian Kershaw calls "a piece of pure theatre." The Nazi leaders who had fought for supremacy while Hitler was in prison all "mounted the platform and, among emotional scenes, with many standing on chairs and tables and the crowd pressing forward from the back of the hall, shook hands, forgave each other, and swore undying loyalty to the leader. It was like medieval vassals swearing fealty to their overlord."[1]

The speech succeeded. Hitler once again was absolute leader of the party.

SPEECH DELIVERED TO A MASS MEETING OF THE NATIONAL SOCIALIST GERMAN WORKERS PARTY

German racial comrades!

I am not speaking to you today to give an account of the past.[2] You received the last report from us on 27 January 1923, at what was then the general membership meeting. We gave you a public accounting of the period up until 8 and 9 November 1923 during the trial.

Today we have another question:

What is to happen in the future?!

I do ask you to listen to me as I give a brief review of the past.

The question of what should happen today can best be answered if we attempt to explain why our movement was founded in the first place.

What were the causes that led to the founding of this new party? Think back to the year 1918. In midsummer, the German people stood at the height of its power. Within a few months it had collapsed, fully defeated, shattered, in ruins.[3] The pressing question back then was: Was there a way out of this deepest misery and misfortune?

Everyone back then asked that question. It even determined the thinking in the minds of those who had perhaps helped to bring about the collapse. In their lucid moments, they, too, asked if and how Germany might one day rise again.

One had to be clear about the fact that the German people faced a great and fateful question, and that the survival or death of our people, for the rest of history, depended on the answer.

The tragedy of our collapse was not the result of military defeat, nor did it result from the terrible peace itself, nor from the oppression that resulted, nor from our lack of weapons and defensive ability, nor even from everything that happened in Germany in the long years that followed. The real tragedy was that everything that happened was our own fault. Up to the very last minute, millions of Germans not only failed to understand, but on the contrary even welcomed, the fact. Hundreds of thousands cheered our defeat, and millions praised the fact that we were without weapons. Others saw our oppression by the enemy as a just judgment, the result of a just punishment. That was the tragic misfortune, the terrible sickness, that afflicted us: a large part of the German people no longer had any sense of the misfortune of their fatherland. That leads us to the fundamental question on which the fate of the German nation will depend: Is it still possible in Germany to reach the masses who no longer believe in their ethnicity, but rather see their brother more in their enemy than in their racial comrades who are of a different party or worldview, and will it be possible to lead this great mass back to a united people's community? Yes or no?

If this question cannot be answered in the right way, the German nation is lost. Peoples can perish. It is nonsense to think that a great people of sixty or seventy million is immortal. It dies if it loses its desire to preserve itself.

Today, eighteen million people in the German Reich still believe that the right of our people to live on this earth does not depend on its survival as such, but rather that it depends on some sort of fantastic opinion coming from others [i.e., Marxism].

Ten million nationally minded people face eighteen or twenty million anti-nationally minded people.

Ten million who are ready to give all for their national heritage, and who always measure justice by the survival of their nation, facing eighteen to twenty million people who have forgotten that.

That is the misery of the German people. As long as this condition lasts and endures, to believe in renewed freedom for the German people is utopian.

Why?

First, what was the real reason for our collapse?

We collapsed because for years during the old Reich, we committed serious domestic sins. We denied the Reich the means it needed to maintain itself. We collapsed because for a long time we entrusted the holiest matters of the whole nation to parliamentary maneuvering, because millions were no longer ready and willing to give their all for the preservation of their own nation and fatherland, but rather were determined to sacrifice their nation and their fatherland for the existence of their party.

We collapsed because the overwhelming majority of citizens was pacifist, anti-national, and Marxist, unwilling to give the state what it needed to preserve itself.

Second, we collapsed internationally, since those abroad knew our domestic weaknesses only too well. They knew the Achilles Heel of the German Reich, knowing only too well the balance of power in parliament. They knew well that any policy of active self-preservation would fail against the majority of half-heartedness, cowardice, and stupidity in this land.

Today, just as in 1918, the question is this: Can this condition be changed?

After the revolution in 1918, any attempt to revive Germany seemed hopeless.

Internationally, Germany had fallen from its former heights, and at home it was torn apart. Almost the entire economy gradually came under the control of foreigners.

Any thinking person back then had to realize that, if these developments continued, Germany would surely perish from international poisoning.

There no longer seemed any hope of improvement. One had to ask if anyone was able to break the hold of this international power over the broad masses. My German racial comrades, the organized power of the International reached from the left wing of the Center Party to the most left wing of Marxism. Only a very weak political force stood against it: the German bourgeoisie.

Why could the bourgeois parties, relatively small in numbers and size, and which lacked energy and an attacking spirit both in 1918 and afterwards, no longer change the situation?

I will briefly give you the reasons.

First, the recognition of the principle of majority rule in parliament ensured that only a majority of people could change things.

The bourgeois parties, however, could no longer win such a majority.

They themselves did not have a majority, for the bourgeoisie organized themselves primarily according to their intellectual and material standing, by how much they owned and how intelligent they were. Only a minority in the world have either. A political movement based on these two foundations must remain in the minority, and is therefore condemned to insignificance in a system in which the majority alone has power.

Second, the path to power was forever closed to the bourgeois parties, since the sins of the fathers were visited on the children. What earlier generations ruined over long decades became the cause for the eternal desire for revenge. For a long time, the misery of the broad masses was ignored. Nobody worried about them. For years, no one saw the injustice. Ask yourself: Sixty or seventy years ago, what party worried about these people? Which party went into the factories, the workplaces, or the streets?

No one from the bourgeois movements.

They all avoided the broad masses. Only when the masses began to organize themselves politically to win equal rights, and Jewry cleverly took control, did those on the political right begin to see that a new power within the state had begun to assert itself, a new, fourth class.

For too many decades, they had not noticed these racial comrades. They did not know them, and had lost any instinct for understanding them. The result was that an unbridgeable chasm developed within the German people that would inevitably lead to disaster. Snobbery on the one side faced organized class insanity on the other. Snobbery can lead only to organized class thinking on the other side. The masses were systematically incited by those people who, by God, had no desire to bring blessings to the masses, but rather saw the masses only as a way to advance their own interests.

The same Jew who on the one side gifted the bourgeoisie with the worst customs, this same Jew now whipped up and agitated the masses, and he took each mistake that either side committed and presented it to the other in a manner distorted and magnified a thousand-fold.

The same Jew, as a capitalist tyrant, drove the masses to desperation, and then exploited this desperation on the other side until the masses were finally ready to be his instrument.

But the bourgeoisie lacked one other thing that is necessary to win over the masses. And that is the most important reason why it never found contact with its people.

The key to the hearts of the masses is not begging, but rather strength.

It lacked the strength that is alone able to win over the masses of a people, namely fanatic faith and fanatic conviction, the relentless pursuit of an ideal, and above all the knowledge that when one is pursuing a just cause, duty requires one to use every means one has.

The bourgeois parties are born clubs of pacifists. That means that they lack not only the strength to attack and the will to attack, but also any ability to attack. He who desires to change a situation has to attack himself, not wait until he is attacked. That was the greatest failing of these bourgeois-political organized movements. They never attacked, but rather were always happy when they were not themselves attacked.

They never had the courage to say: "There is our goal, there is the enemy. Down with him. Only when the last of our enemies has been defeated is our victory sure."

No, no. They were satisfied if fate did not treat them too unkindly in the next Reichstag election, if they were able to save a dozen seats, and they hoped that in the end, maybe their opponent in the coming years would make mistakes as big as they had made, so that the people would weary of them and the movement could win nine new seats, which would be a tremendous success.

That is what these movements were fighting for.

Of course, they were unable to attack. They were too tied to their possessions, whether intellectual or material, which always weakens the will to attack.

But they wanted nothing more. They were too "well brought up," too "refined."

The bad smells of a mass meeting make these gentlemen uncomfortable.

They do not love beer halls, and still find it unpleasant today when the beer halls begin to consider larger issues, although one might ask which is really the better of the two, a parliamentary meeting room or a beer hall.

They are too refined to attack.

And finally, they are unable to attack because they are led by the same power that leads their opponents.

Do you really believe that any of these bourgeois movements, always led from behind the scenes by Hebrews, could ever find the strength to attack the left, which is, of course, a brother party of a different color?!

No, dear God, no!

They shake each others' hands and get along well enough. Only during elections is there a battle, never one about principles, but rather only a stink about seats in parliament.

They would welcome a way to avoid battle, were there a way that seemed reasonable, if the left was agreeable. But it wants a fight.

But the most important reason that the bourgeoisie could never win over the masses was that its political movements had no fundamentally new worldview.

My German racial comrades, that is the most significant and important fact. When a movement is fighting to advance, and when it has a certain goal, that goal also gives the movement a milestone that everyone can see. One knows one has been successful when it reaches this goal. That does not end a struggle prematurely, for the movement will be driven on to new goals.

The situation is the opposite when one is on the defensive. One is passive. Who can say when the goal has been reached? In the most favorable situation, when a position seems secure. That is the difference between the bourgeois parties and those to the left: the bourgeois movements fight to keep what they have; the left fights for the victory of its program, for the realization of its goals.

This goal, however, is the collapse of the fatherland, the destruction of the nation, the ruination of the national economy, and the establishment of international Jewish financial hegemony.

That was the weakness of Germany's political bourgeoisie. It had nothing to offer to combat the other side's brutal goal of destroying all values, including that of race.

For that reason, the bourgeois battle against Marxism was doomed to fail.

However, we must all realize this: Marxism, whether in the form of social democracy or communism, can be defeated as long as it faces a doctrine of greater truthfulness, but with the same brutal methods.

Such a doctrine, however, must always be rooted in the broad masses. Only there can one find the resolute fighters who are ready to give all for their ideals. The broad masses are not so rich in intellectual or material possessions as to keep them from fighting for a distant goal.

Only the broad masses move forward, only they are willing to sacrifice. Therefore, every movement on earth that is not rooted in them is doomed to failure. Each movement, on the other hand, that reaches, gathers, and organizes the lower classes, and leads them to battle, can and will be victorious.

The Jew understood this, and that is why he organized the broad masses. That is why, even though he avoids all practical labor, he went into the factories to lie and lie, and since he is the virtuoso of lies, finally succeeded in presenting himself as a benefactor of the masses. He brought them together, learned their wishes, and promised the satisfaction of every wish, thus forging an army of millions of strong fists that he then used his intelligence to lead. The Jew, in brilliant ways, saw what the bourgeoisie had overlooked.

He understood that earth-shaking ideas can only be realized if they are supported by millions of people in the lower classes of a people. Cleverly and systematically, he transformed this idea into reality by organizing countless workers and thus forged a powerful mass of people together, using them to destroy the backbone of the national state, to ruin the national economy, to wipe out its racial foundations, and to establish his dictatorship.

I ask you: Do you believe that this situation will change by chance, or do you believe that when one sees inevitable catastrophe coming, one has the duty, the right, to demand of each individual that he fight against it with all the strength at his command, even in the end to go on the attack himself?

That is what moved us all back then when we founded the National Socialist German Workers Party.

The goal then was clear and simple: To fight the devil's forces that had plunged Germany into this misery, to fight Marxism along with the other intellectual carriers of this world plague and epidemic, the Jews. We did not want to fight in the bourgeois manner, "carefully," so that one does not get hurt. No, and no again!

As we joined together in this new movement, one thing was clear to us. There were only two possible outcomes: either the enemy would walk over our corpses, or we would walk over his.

The battle against the world plague would not be won by gaining several seats in parliament, but rather it would be assured only when the swastika flag flew over the last workplace and the last factory, and the last Soviet star, whether open or concealed, had disappeared.

From the very first days, we knew that the movement had to follow two principles:

To make a cause understandable to the broad masses, one must fight both it and the people who represent it. Remember England's brilliant propaganda preparations for the war against us. Whom did England fight against? The person of the German Kaiser, and against militarism.

Whom is Jewry fighting through its Marxist forces? Against the bourgeoisie as individuals, and against "capitalism."

Who was our movement to fight? Against the Jew as a person, and against Marxism.

There were several practical requirements:

First, we had to concentrate the whole strength of the movement on a single goal, and that for pragmatic reasons.

If one wants to accomplish an important goal, one must have the masses on his side. But the mass of people is infinitely varied. Each individual has certain opinions, certain abilities, a certain temperament, a liking for some things and a dislike for others. It is hard enough to find a goal for 10,000 people, but even harder to find a goal for these 10,000 that consists of sixteen or twenty smaller goals. Imagine that you stand before a small group and say: "We are fighting the Jews and the Marxists." The group will perhaps go along with you. Now imagine a second goal: "We are fighting for this or that as well." Now, that will offend someone or other, who will say: "I cannot go along with that." If you now add a third goal, someone else will object, and so on if you add a fourth, and so on. Once you have a list of twenty goals, there may be five people left who agree with all twenty goals. Therefore, it is pragmatically necessary to focus on one goal, unifying as large a mass of people as possible behind it, and with them begin a unified attack.

Second, it is psychologically wrong to set several goals. A person is inclined to look for reasons in every instance. The German people, especially inclined to hyper-objectivity, is always ready to ask: Do I have the right to do that? Or does my opponent have more justice on his side than I do?

Look around Germany today and pick ten enemies as your target. Ninety of a hundred Germans immediately will say: "Can these ten all be wrong, and only us right?" If you pick twenty goals, people will be even more tortured by the question: "Everyone else is wrong, and only we are right?" Our people always looks to the rights of others, not to its own self-preservation. To the degree that you add goals, the confidence, the faith of the individual sinks, hurting the strongest foundation that a person can have, namely the conviction that he is fighting for justice.

That is the issue. If human beings and peoples are to be strong, they must be convinced that they are fighting for an entirely just cause. That is why it is necessary to have only a few goals, and to choose an enemy that everyone can see.

There is the guilty one, him alone.

The Allies understood that brilliantly. They did not say that they were fighting Germany, Austria, Bulgaria, Turkey, and so forth, but rather they always said: "We are fighting only the Kaiser and militarism." Whether they were fighting in Mesopotamia, Russia, France, Serbia, or somewhere else, it was always the Kaiser and militarism. That is how they brought twenty-six states into the war against Germany. Imagine how that strengthened the confidence of each Englishman! He could tell himself: "Can we be wrong when it is twenty-six against one?" On our side, on the other hand, the average man could ask: "Can we be right when twenty-six are against us? Can all twenty-six be wrong?"

Believe me, particularly with a people like the Germans, it is absolutely necessary, for psychological reasons, to pick one enemy and march against him. When necessary, one can mean several enemies when referring to one. Besides these two reasons for focusing on one enemy, there are others. The most important one is that this goal is a vital question of survival for the German nation. Do not be deceived by the dangers that people always try to present as more pressing ones.

The greatest danger we face is and remains the poison of foreign peoples in our national body. All other dangers are of limited duration. Only this one has eternal consequences. Many are speaking of new goals for the movement, and fail to see the forest for the trees. They suddenly believe that it is necessary to fight fifteen or twenty opponents. In the midst of this confusion of goals, I ask you only to think of Berlin, to look at Friedrichstraße. There you will see one Jewish lad after another with his arm around a German girl. Then remember that every night, thousands and thousands of people of our blood are destroyed forever in a single moment, their children and grandchildren lost to us.

And remember this: One can break peace treaties. Reparations agreements can be cancelled or rejected. Political parties can be dealt with. But blood that has once been poisoned cannot be changed. It remains, it spreads, and harms us more and more each year. If you wonder about the current fragmentation of our people, remember this: The inner discord of the German people is the result only of mixed blood.

That is the greatest danger. If this poisoning continues, we will be weaker in ten, twenty, or thirty years than we are today, weaker in a hundred years than we will be in thirty, weaker in two hundred years than we will be in one hundred, and the time will come when our people loses its high cultural standing, and we will perish from blood poisoning. Everything beautiful that we see around us is the result of the Aryan, of his spirit and industry. Only the bad is the gift of the Hebrews.

And we will lose the strength we will need to rebuild not only in the cultural, but also in the physical realm.

If the German people does not master this plague, it will perish from it.

The art of great popular leaders has always been to concentrate the attention of the masses on one enemy. Only thus can one build the surge of passion necessary for every major success. Believe me when I say that the understanding plays only a minor role here. The right feeling is more important than all understanding. Understanding can deceive people; sure feeling never does. It is not by chance that you see so many women in our movement and here in this hall, even though our movement fights in the most manly way. You see them here because feelings dominate in women, and tell women: "The future of our children is at stake, and therefore the future of our race." Then there is no wavering, no confusion the next day when some bookworm invents some scientific reason to the contrary. No, feelings are stable. They do not waver or weaken.

A certain Dr. Heim may talk about our "hysterical women." Women brought Christianity to the nations, and will also, in the end, lead our movement to lasting victory. If she is not there, not only the woman is lacking, but also the youth, and therefore the future. You can be sure that the movement with the fewest women also has the least strength. That is why, for example, you find only a few "ladies" in the democratic parties.

If one agrees that a movement has to pursue one goal, he must also agree that everything has to be subject to a single thought. This should be symbolically expressed in its name. That is why we chose the name "National Socialist German Workers Party."

We chose "National Socialist" because the supreme goal of the movement embodies the connection between living national strength and the purest social goals. We were convinced that the hearts of the masses could never be won through shouting "Heil" alone; they had to be persuaded that our people's movement was interested in each individual, and that we were not handing out gifts, but rather that we wanted to establish justice. And that we saw the future of our people not in a one-sided highly bred intelligentsia, but rather in a healthy people.

And we are a German workers' party. We welcome only those who are not ashamed to say: "I, too, am a worker, a productive human being." He who cannot say this word with respect, by God, has not yet learned how to be the best sort of German.

And that is why we chose the swastika as our symbol, on a white circle against a red background. This symbol emphasized our single goal. The swastika is a symbol of labor, the white a symbol of our national sentiments, and the red a symbol of our true socialist thinking. The cross, however, has still another meaning: the spirit of labor on this earth, which is the spirit of Aryan idealism, not the spirit of the Jew.

It is, therefore, the symbol under which we fight this world plague, this world poisoning.

Our attitude toward parliament flowed from this attitude.

Why did we reject parliament back then? The young movement wanted to train fighters, not become parliamentarians. The movement was convinced that it was too early to go into such places. It thought that, just as today, we needed speakers, agitators, and apostles to speak to the masses to spread the new doctrine, to attempt to win over the masses, to organize them, to win new strongholds to strengthen and expand the movement.

Our program was to be a logical expansion of this tendency. It was a guiding star, freeing us from the question: "What do you want to do tomorrow or the day after tomorrow?" It was to determine the direction of the movement for decades to come. Its ideas were ethical, immortal, imperishable, able to enlighten people in distant centuries. The carriers of these ideas, however, had to be human. We knew even then that the battle against Jewry could not be fought only against the race as such, but also against its living manifestation, individual persons. That is why we set the faith in the value of personality over against the Jewish thinking of majority rule.

That is how our movement began its labors. It wanted to do what the bourgeois parties had failed to do. Above all, it wanted to reach the masses, spreading true national feelings.

You know how well it succeeded. We began with nothing. Four and a half years later, our movement's name was on everyone's lips. The whole world has heard about us since then.

Then the tragic day came. You all know about it. On that bitter day, for the first time in the history of the young movement, people perished, thereby proving in the most vivid way their sacrificial spirit. The movement itself was banned, its organizations dissolved. Only through hard effort did some attempt to continue the work, and many, many, went to prison.

A year has passed, and the movement is once again free. It is again free, which means we have the opportunity to rebuild everything again, or to give up. Do not be surprised that I see only one way to proceed.

Why am I calling the old movement, the old party, to life once again?

You know that there is evil, bitter strife today. Do not ask me to take sides in this strife. Even today, I still see each party member as a supporter of our common idea. Even today, I still see not the individual before me, but rather a great thought. If I fall into doubt, I need only to close my eyes to see before me the hour in which thousands were ready, if necessary, to die for this idea. Do not believe that I have forsaken this idea. It is my unshakable guiding star, now and forever. Anyone whom I believe shares even a part of this thinking is, in my eyes, my brother, and belongs once more in the old ranks. I do not see my task as leader of the new movement to investigate, to inquire, or to study the past. I see only one duty, namely to bring those who have gone different ways back together again. I could not do that were I to take sides in party conflicts.

Therefore I have taken up the old flag once more, confident that it will bring together once more all those who share our thinking. The old flag must succeed once again in forming a single great, living movement from the chaos we find ourselves in today. The old flag must again bring together the competing leaders, and convince the masses that the movement is not dying, but rather that it is just beginning today.

We have to do that today.

More than ever before, the fate of Germany calls to us: "Germans, be on guard and defend yourselves." Our people has slumbered over these last months. It will either have a rude awakening, or it will not wake up at all. The old parties are rapidly collapsing. What are they fighting for? For ridiculous goals. How weak they are! They fight about everything. Are they to lead the German nation?

How long can a people survive this situation? I know that many feel this misery only when it affects their own pocket books. Believe me, that will happen again. The deceptive foundation of our current economy will vanish, and then people will perhaps understand what we are saying better than they do today. We need to remind people that when they were not worried in the past, we were already prophesying what would come to pass.

Now, my dear party comrades, I come to a series of matters of principle. When yesterday I raised the flag of our old movement, I expected that all those who in their hearts had remained National Socialists would flock to me. I am not concerned about the great masses as such. In the past, I swam against the powerful current for a long time. It is the same today. Whoever does not want to join our camp can stay away. But to whomever wishes to join us, I say: "The bickering is over."

Do not come to me with reasons to keep it up. Do not come to me and say: "I can do everything except this or that, and so-and-so has done so many things wrong that I can never. . . ." No, let he who is without sin cast the first stone, but then have the courage to throw one at me, too, for like every one of you, I have made mistakes. No one has the right to beat his breast and say: "He is to blame, but I am as pure as the angels."

He who thinks that way is the guiltiest. He is unjust, and deceives himself.

Today people talk a lot about "cooperating." The first prerequisite for cooperation is mutual understanding. The first prerequisite for understanding is forgiveness. And he who cannot forgive, in my eyes, is not worthy of being part of our movement.

Do not come to me and say: "Yeah, sure, but my opinion is in the interests of the movement."

Gentlemen, from now on, let me worry about the interests of the movement!

You had nine months to protect the interests of the movement. Many times in my cell, I spent sleepless nights pacing back and forth, worrying about how the interests of the movement were being protected.

I therefore ask that from now on, everyone follow the path that I want to, and will, show him.

I am not standing here to complain about someone, to insult someone, or to make some sort of mild reproach to anyone. I ask but one thing of you: Join the ranks of the old movement again and leave everything from the past in the past.

I ask you to remember the great sacrifices many have made for the movement. I believe that, were the earth to give back those who fell on 9 November, they would stand beside me now and say to you: "We did not want this strife. We did not die for individuals, but for our great, common faith and for our common labors."

I speak above all to our German youth.

You do not know if you will one day have to fight again for the freedom of the German fatherland. If you wish once again to visit the Rhine,[4] do not go as individuals; rather, march together shoulder to shoulder. Do that now in our movement as well!

I turn to women. I ask you to be ruled by a single feeling: the feeling of obligation, which is the greatest treasure that we have. Care for it, preserve it, do not let it fall into the gutter. Every harsh word that we say to each other will be a weapon that our enemies can use against us.

I believe that we have a symbol that can appeal to everyone. Our old flag has rested these last fifteen months. Today it flies once more, and each can swear his oath to it once more. Everyone can join our ranks again. He who cannot do this can go his own way.

Whoever thinks that he can join us with "conditions" does not know me very well. For nine months, I said nothing. Now I lead the movement, and no one can ask for conditions from me. If a person comes to me and says I have this condition, and someone else comes to me with another condition, I have but one answer: "My friend, wait until I make the conditions."

I am not willing to be restricted by conditions as long as I bear the responsibility. And once again, I bear the responsibility for everything that happens in this movement.

Once again, I ask you to put aside everything that separates us, and remember that today, all of Germany is looking toward us. There are only three or four thousand of us in this hall. But in a short while, two or three million must grow from these four thousand.

The movement is entering a new year.

I will call a provisional membership meeting and it will elect the leadership. In the next year, we will then hold the first regular membership meeting. I ask you to refrain from all criticism until then, including criticism of me. We will see each other again in a year, and then you may judge. If I have done well, do not criticize me any longer. And if I have done badly, I will surrender my office back to you. I believe I can promise you today, however, that our movement will come to life again. I believe in our old flag. I designed it myself. I was the first to carry it. And my only wish is that, when the grim reaper finally strikes me down, that it will be my burial shroud. And I believe that you, too, do not want to desert this old flag, that you cannot desert it.

Times today are grim.

Our people dances while death nears. Our task is to walk into the swamp once more and tell people what they must be told. I believe that many eyes can be opened in the coming year. Many will see through the deceptive veil, and people who curse us today will be new fighters in our ranks. To win these people is your most important task.

ADOLF HITLER

Forget all internal bickering, even if others attack me. That is irrelevant. We do not want to fight about it.

What we want to do is to reach the masses, to rescue them from their present insanity, and bring them back to their ethnic roots, so that one day Germany will rise once more under our flag.

That great thing, not the party, is our goal.

When we put away our disagreements, we can more easily join in the ideal that binds us together, in a common value, our common, holy German fatherland.

NOTES

1. Ian Kershaw, *Hitler 1889–1936: Hubris* (New York: W. W. Norton, 1998), 267.

2. The source: *Die Rede Adolf Hitlers in der ersten großen Massenversammlung (Münchener Bürgerbräu-Keller vom 27 Februar 1925) bei der Wiederaufrichtung der Nationalsozialistischen Deutschen Arbeiter-Partei* (Munich: Franz Eher, 1925).

3. The Nazis argued that Germany had lost World War I not on the battlefield, but because it had been "stabbed in the back" by traitors within Germany. Although the argument was false, Germans found it plausible, since even in November 1918, when Germany agreed to an armistice, its armies were still on foreign soil.

4. German territory along the Rhine River was a demilitarized zone under a provision of the Treaty of Versailles.

Joseph Goebbels

"The Storm Is Coming"

9 July 1932

Hitler sent Joseph Goebbels (1897–1945) to Berlin in 1926 to take charge of an ineffective party organization in Germany's capital. Goebbels set to work, speaking widely and establishing a weekly newspaper titled *Der Angriff* (The Attack). He quickly made the Nazis visible in Berlin.

In 1930, Hitler made Goebbels the director of the party propaganda system, a position he held until 1945. He had a leading role in directing Nazi election campaigns before Hitler's takeover of power. In 1928, the Nazis had won only twelve seats in the *Reichstag,* the German parliament. Then the Great Depression fell hard on Germany. In 1930, the Nazis won 107 seats, becoming the second largest party. Political and economic chaos led to four nationwide election campaigns in 1932: a presidential election, a run-off between the two top candidates, Hitler and Hindenburg, and two *Reichstag* elections. Goebbels had a central role in them all.

He was also one of the party's most effective speakers, regularly standing before mass audiences throughout Germany. This speech was delivered to a huge outdoor meeting in Berlin three weeks before the first of the 1932 *Reichstag* elections, in which the Nazis would win 230 seats, making them the largest German political party. Goebbels evidently thought this one of the best of his pre-1933 speeches, since it is one of the few he reprinted in his later books.

Goebbels's rhetoric typifies the style of Nazi campaign speaking. Hitler had written in *Mein Kampf* that political propaganda was based on simplicity, repetition, and emotional appeal. Goebbels made these principles central to Nazi propaganda in general, and his own speaking in particular.

Goebbels does not explain what the Nazis will do once in power, but rather vehemently attacks the existing government, and promises that the Nazis will do better. As he once explained to his fellow propagandists, one could argue for ten years in favor of educational reform and get nowhere, but if one fought for and gained political power, one could change the educational system (and everything else) immediately.

In his published diary of the period, calculated to make him appear in the most favorable light, Goebbels claimed that this speech was a great success:

> One hundred thousand people in the Lustgarten. Every inch of room is taken up. Excitement reaches boiling point. Count Helldorf is the first speaker. He at once comes to the point with a vengeance. I then harp on the same string and get in a thrust at the whole Cabinet. The proclamation of war is seized upon by the huge crowd with unparalleled enthusiasm.[1]

The speech may not have been quite that successful—but it is an excellent example of Nazi campaign oratory.

A CAMPAIGN SPEECH

Germans of Berlin!

I am speaking as the representative of the greatest movement of millions ever seen on German soil.[2] I am here not to beg for your vote, your favor, or your forgiveness. I only want you to be just. Give your verdict on the past fourteen years, on its shame, its disgrace, its collapse, and our growing national political humiliation. You must decide if the men and parties that are responsible for these past fourteen years should have the right to continue to hold power in the government.

Comrades, this new system was born fourteen years ago. One

never judges systems or governments by what they want to do or what they promise, but rather always by what they can do, and by what they accomplish. The men of November [1918] took power by lying to the people, by telling them they had won. They promised you, workers, citizens, and creative Germans, a Reich of freedom and beauty and dignity. They promised you socialism, they promised a people's state, they promised the broad masses the fulfillment of their dreams—peace, work, and prosperity.

We have lived this lie for fourteen years. For fourteen years we have worshipped this governmental structure; we have lived in want, suffered, sacrificed, starved, sometimes wept. And now we see the worst results of these fourteen years: the German economy is in ruins, there are huge budget deficits, the nation's whole fortune is squandered, people are robbed of their inheritance, people are desperate and without hope, the streets of our big cities are filled with an army of millions of unemployed, the middle class is vanishing, the farmers driven from their land. To our shame and disgrace, large areas of German territory have been lost. Our territory is divided by the bleeding wound of the Polish Corridor,[3] and Germany is drained by stupid and unnatural tribute payments.

More than that, the red battalions preach civil war and bloody class conflict that are tearing our nation apart, giving the German people no peace. In such a situation, the leaders and parties of the old system are making the hopeless attempt to free Germany from its foreign chains. We go from one conference on reparations to another. We signed Versailles, Dawes, and Young.[4] Each treaty meant more hunger, more torture, more terror, more horror for the suffering German people.

It is not hard to determine who is guilty, who bears the responsibility, to the people, to history, and to God for these conditions. It is those men and the parties who have misled the German people for fourteen years, promising them lives of beauty and dignity, of heaven on earth, but who in the end gave us empty words and stones instead of bread. They stand now before the court of the nation to give an account of the unparalleled disaster they have brought about in the last fourteen years. Five weeks ago, the last cabinet of this system fell. New men came on the political stage and declared that they intended to replace the November System[5]

JOSEPH GOEBBELS

and set Germany on a fundamentally new political course. You men and women know that we viewed this attempt with suspicion from the beginning. We do not see the resurrection of our people as coming from a small clique that has no strong connection to the people; only a movement of millions has the active strength and the ability to change Germany.

What has the new cabinet done in these past five weeks?

It wanted to bring the budget in balance. That was necessary, since the coffers were empty as it took power. But balancing the budget will not solve our problems. The real cause of our need is unemployment. Asking the people to sacrifice makes sense only if that sacrifice is the first step to recovery. What did this so-called cabinet of national concentration do? It relied on the Brüning Emergency Decree,[6] and intensified it. This cabinet cut the meager unemployment compensation, reduced the pensions of war victims, adopted the salt tax, the most unsocial measure. This cabinet should not think that we National Socialists will support its harmful policies.

I ask you, men and women, how can the Social Democratic Party find the gall to accuse us of intolerance, when that is exactly how it behaved during the last two years under Brüning? The Social Democratic Party would be ready to swallow the Emergency Decree if it were assured that the new cabinet would fight our movement as hard as Brüning's government did.

What has changed?

Nothing at all, except that the ruling men have different faces. The economy is running on empty; the government has failed to begin a new job creation program. The misery of the broad masses continues to increase, and those who are starving do not know how they can survive from one day to the next. The middle class is collapsing under heavy taxes and the farmer is leaving his farm because he can no longer pay the interest, mortgage, and debts. All the cabinet can say is this: "We cannot fix in five weeks what went wrong in fourteen years!" Well, OK! But one should at least be able to see that a start is being made. We agree that not much can be done with Article 48.[7] But at least we should be able to expect that the government would be making attempts to resolve the political problems we face. But what do we see?

Red murder rages through the streets. Barricades are built in Moabit.[8] Every evening fifty, sixty, or seventy of our members are seriously wounded, and every day we bury one or two or three comrades. The lying Red press is more active than ever, and in the south and west of Germany the Center Party and its ecclesiastical cousin, the Bavarian People's Party, threaten a splintering of the Reich.

What is the Reich interior minister doing about it?

He sits with his hands in his lap. He wants to treat the right and the left impartially, but thereby treats us unjustly. You, my comrades, stand here in your worn-out brown uniforms. The government has allowed you to be slandered, and your uniforms are paid for by the contributions of the poor. The government has not fallen wholly into the arms of the Reds. It claims to be national, but we are convinced that were it not for us National Socialists, this weak government would long have used up the capital that national Germany has built up over a twelve-year struggle for rebirth.

A new Germany has arisen! It is a Germany that has fought for twelve years against Marxist betrayal and bourgeois weakness.

You, men, women, and comrades, are the bearers, witnesses, builders, and finishers of this unique people's uprising. Our policies have not been popular. We have served the truth, and only the truth. For twelve years, they have insulted and outlawed and slandered and persecuted us. Now that we are standing at the doorway to power, Marxist lies have joined with bourgeois weakness to fight us. Were we only a party like all the rest, we would collapse under our opponents' offensive. But we are a people's movement. That is our good fortune. Here and everywhere else in the land, the red shining swastika flag flies over people of all camps, parties, classes, occupations, and religious confessions. Our opponents laughed at us in the past, but they laugh no longer.

You men and women standing before me, a hundred or two hundred thousand in number, with heads high, upright, proud, and brave, the carriers of Germany's future, in your eyes it is written: We think no longer in terms of class. We are not workers or middle class. We are not first of all Protestants or Catholics. We do not ask about ancestry or class. Together we share the words of the poet:

"Now, people rise up, and storm, break loose!"

Comrades, men and women, fate has given us a last chance. We have one more opportunity to speak to the people. Our campaign spreads to all of Germany, and once again the ears hear, the eyes see, the heart beats faster, and the senses clear:

"The day of freedom and prosperity is coming!"

So our dead comrade Horst Wessel wrote, and we are fulfilling his prophesy.[9] The others may lie, slander, and pour their scorn on us—their political days are numbered.

Adolf Hitler is knocking at the gates of power, and in his fist are joined the fists of millions of workers and farmers. The time of shame and disgrace is nearly over.

You are the witnesses, the builders, the will-bearers of our idea and our worldview.

The party hacks of the Socialist Party are suddenly remembering the people. For a decade, the illustrated magazines pictured them only in frock coats and cylinder hats at tables filled with oysters and champagne bottles. Now they wear workers' caps and fill their newspapers with urgings like "People, wake up!"

Well, we the people have awakened! We have risen against oppression; fifteen million people have joined in an army of revenge. They who accepted their nice suits from the Sklareks[10] can hardly imagine that an honest German worker will spend his starvation wages for a decent brown shirt. They who have grown fat on caviar, who are paid seventy or eighty or a hundred thousand marks a year, who have spread the stink of unprecedented corruption over all of Germany, they want to pretend they are an opposition. "To the barricades!" they cry.

Our answer: "The good old days of party bigwigs are over. A new Germany is coming, a Germany raised on the Spartan laws of Prussian duty. It is a Germany not grown fat, but one that is starving! It is a Germany with strength, with will, with idealism! It is a Germany that is done with Marxist betrayal and bourgeois white gloves."

And you, the people, are the witnesses of this Germany. You, the people, have affirmed this Germany. And we speak in your name. We, the leaders of this exciting movement of millions, we come from you, the people. We, too, comrades, were once unknown men marching with the gray masses. People, we have shared in our hearts your torture, your misery, your tribulations, your desperation. We are a part of the people. When the bourgeois know-it-alls ask what we have accomplished, you, men and women, must save us from the necessity of giving answer. When they ask what we have done, you fifteen million must answer: "They have given us faith once more, they have given us hope. They have awakened a sleeping Germany. They have organized and mobilized millions and set them to march." These millions are in motion, following the laws of history. Just as this small sect grew from seven unknown men to a movement of fifteen million, so, too, and this I swear to you, will this movement of fifteen million grow to encompass a people of sixty-five million.

The parties must go! The political hacks must be thrown out of their seats. We will give no pardon. We will not allow Germany to sink into disgrace. We will give back to Germany a reason for its existence, a meaning to life. That is why you men and women are here, an army of two hundred thousand. Never has the Reich capital seen a popular movement of such force. You have come here from everywhere. The middle class has come from the west, the workers from the east and north. You have come from dark and joyless apartment houses. My S.A. comrades[11] are before me, heads high, as if they were the kings of Germany. I know, comrades, that there are some among you who do not know where tomorrow's meal will come from. We have shown those materialist party hacks that idealism is alive in Germany. We have shown those materialistic bigwigs that even in the midst of hunger, sacrifice, and need, the people can be shown the way to betterment. We pledge loyalty to this people. We solemnly raise our hands and pledge:

As long as we breathe, we are obligated to the German people. We came from the people, and return ever to it. The people is the center of all things to us. We sacrifice for this people, and if necessary are ready to die for it.

Loyalty to the people, loyalty to the idea, loyalty to the movement, and loyalty to the Führer! That is our oath as we shout:

Our Führer and our party—Hail victory!

1. Joseph Goebbels, *Vom Kaiserhof zur Reichskanzlei* (Munich: Franz Eher, 1934).

2. The text is in Joseph Goebbels, *Signale der neuen Zeit* (Munich: Franz Eher, 1938), 82–90.

3. Under the Treaty of Versailles, Poland was given former German territory to provide it with a route to the sea.

4. The Dawes and Young Plans were international agreements on German reparations payments for World War I.

5. The Nazi term for the German government established after World War I.

6. The German constitution allowed the chancellor to rule by decree when the *Reichstag* was unable to agree on a government coalition.

7. The constitutional provision that allowed government by presidential decree.

8. A working class district of Berlin.

9. Horst Wessel, a Berlin Nazi murdered by a communist as the result of a dispute about a prostitute, wrote the text of what became the Nazi Party's anthem.

10. Jewish brothers who were involved in a major Berlin financial scandal.

11. The S.A., or Storm Troop, was a Nazi paramilitary group that often fought political opponents on the streets and in political meetings.

Joseph Goebbels

*Propaganda and Public Enlightenment as
Prerequisites for Practical Work in Many Areas*

6 SEPTEMBER 1934

In the United States, propaganda was, and remains, a dirty word.
Not so to the Nazis. Two months after Hitler took power, he ap-
pointed Goebbels to head the newly established Ministry for
Public Enlightenment and Propaganda. Goebbels argued that
the methods of propaganda are morally neutral. There was no
such thing as inherently "good" propaganda or "bad" propaganda
methods. The criterion is whether or not propaganda is used for
good ends.

In this speech, given at the 1934 Nuremberg Party Rally, Goebbels presents propaganda as invaluable in the service of party and
state. He repeats the Nazi explanation of why Germany had lost
World War I. Rather than losing it on the battlefield, he argued
that Germany lost the war of propaganda, being defeated only because morale collapsed at home. This was an attractive argument.
First, it sounded plausible. After all, when Germany asked for an
armistice in November 1918, its armies were still deep in France,
and it had defeated Russia the year before. What Germans at the
time did not realize was that their military was exhausted, and
that the rising contributions of the United States to the Allied war
effort made German defeat inevitable. Second, it preserved the
myth of the German military—it had not lost the war, it had been
betrayed. During World War II, the Nazis repeatedly argued that
Germany would not again be tricked into giving up the battle just
before victory.

Goebbels also presents Nazi propaganda as truthful. Good propaganda, he says, does not need to lie, In fact, it may not lie. Although Goebbels was entirely willing to lie when he thought it necessary, he also knew the dangers of making false claims. He, and Nazi propaganda in general, preferred to mislead by selection or omission rather than by outright falsification.

The major part of the speech presents propaganda as a noble art. The German people, he suggests, will support everything the Nazis want to do, as long as it is presented to them in the right way. He refers to the "Winter Relief" campaign. This was the Nazi party's charity drive. It did have genuine public support. However, there was also significant pressure to donate. For example, party members solicited contributions, giving a badge to those who had contributed. Those not wearing a badge stood out. He also cites two referendums that Hitler held in 1933 and 1934. In both cases, 90 percent or more people voted "yes." Hitler did enjoy widespread support, but there was also strong pressure on people to vote as expected. And in neither case was there a real campaign. No one argued in public against a "yes" vote. Goebbels entirely ignores the unsavory side of National Socialism. There is one passing mention of the Jews, and he ignores the critical role of force in propaganda (as he wrote in his diaries, "a sharp sword stands behind all effective propaganda").

This speech is most famous because of its concluding words, which are featured in Leni Riefenstahl's film of the 1934 Nuremberg Rally, *Triumph of the Will.*

SPEECH TO THE 1934 NUREMBURG PARTY RALLY

It is difficult to define the concept of propaganda thoroughly and precisely.[1] This is especially true because, in past decades, it was subject to unfavorable, and in part extraordinarily hostile, definitions by us Germans. First, then, we must defend it. Those abroad frequently claim that in the past we Germans were particularly knowledgeable in this area, and knew how to apply it, but that unfortunately is not consistent with the facts. We learned the consequences of our neglect all too clearly during the World War.

While the enemy states produced unprecedented atrocity propaganda aimed at Germany throughout the whole world, we did nothing and were completely defenseless against it. Only when enemy foreign propaganda had nearly won over the greater part even of the neutral states did the German government begin to sense the enormous power of propaganda. It was too late. Just as we were militarily and economically unprepared for the war, so, too, with propaganda. We lost the war in this area more than in any other.

The cleverest trick used in propaganda against Germany during the war was to accuse Germany of what our enemies themselves were doing. Even today, large parts of world opinion are convinced that the typical characteristics of German propaganda are lying, crudeness, reversing the facts, and the like. One needs only to remember the stories that were spread throughout the world at the beginning of the war about German soldiers chopping off children's hands and crucifying women to realize that Germany then was a defenseless victim of this campaign of calumny. It neither had nor used any means of defense.

The concept of propaganda has undergone a fundamental transformation, particularly as the result of political practice in Germany. Throughout the world today, people are beginning to see that a modern state, whether democratic or authoritarian, cannot withstand the subterranean forces of anarchy and chaos without propaganda. It is not only a matter of doing the right thing; the people must understand that the right thing is the right thing. Propaganda includes everything that helps the people to realize this.

Political propaganda in principle is active and revolutionary. It is aimed at the broad masses. It speaks the language of the people because it wants to be understood by the people. Its task is the highest creative art of putting sometimes complicated events and facts in a way simple enough to be understood by the man on the street. Its foundation is that there is nothing the people cannot understand; things must only be put in a way that it can understand. It is a question of making it clear by using the proper approach, evidence, and language.

Propaganda is a means to an end. Its purpose is to lead the people to an understanding that will allow it to willingly and without internal resistance devote itself to the tasks and goals of the leadership. If propaganda is to succeed, it must know what it wants. It must keep a clear and firm goal in mind, and seek the appropriate means and methods to reach that goal. Propaganda as such is neither good nor evil. Its moral value is determined by the goals it seeks.

Propaganda must be creative. It is by no means a matter for the bureaucracy or governmental administration, but rather it is a matter of productive creativity. The genuine propagandist must be a true artist. He must be a master of the people's soul, using it as an instrument to express the majesty of a genuine and unified political will. Propaganda can be pro or con. In neither case does it have to be negative. The only thing that is important is whether or not its words are true and genuine expressions of a people's values. During its period of opposition, the National Socialist movement proved that criticism can be constructive, indeed, that in a time which the government is in the hands of destructive powers it may be the only constructive element.

The concept of public education is fundamentally different. It is basically defensive and evolutionary. It does not hammer or drum. It is moderate in tone, seeking to teach. It explains, clarifies, and informs. It is, therefore, used more often by a government than by the opposition. The National Socialist state, growing out of a revolution, had the task of centrally leading both propaganda and education, uniting two concepts that are related but not identical, molding them into a unity that in the long term can serve the government and people.

Even during the time when we were in the opposition, we succeeded in rescuing the concept of propaganda from disfavor or contempt. Since then, we have transformed it into a truly creative art. It was our sharpest weapon in conquering the state. It remains our sharpest weapon in defending and building the state. Although this is perhaps still not clear to the rest of the world, it was obvious to us that we had to use the weapon with which we had conquered the state to defend the state. Otherwise we faced the danger that we could lose the people even though we had power, and that, without the people, we would lose power. We put what we had learned during our attack on the November pseudo-state in the service of our state. The great wealth of ideas and never failing creativity of our propaganda, proven during our struggle for power, was perfected to the last detail. Now we turned it to serve the state itself, to find meaningful and flexible ways to influence the people's thinking. The people should share the concerns and successes of its government. These concerns and successes must therefore be constantly presented and hammered into the people so that it will consider the concerns and successes of its government to be its concerns and successes. Only an authoritarian government, firmly tied to a people, can do this over the long term. Political propaganda, the art of anchoring the things of the state in the broad masses so that the whole nation will feel a part of them, cannot therefore remain merely a means to the goal of winning power. It must become a means of building and keeping power.

This requires alert attention to the events of the day, and a trained and lively creativity that must include a complete knowledge of the soul of a people. A people must be understood in its deepest depths, or intuitively understood, for only then can one speak in a way that a people will understand. Propaganda must be the science of the soul of a people. It requires an organized and purposeful system if it is to be successful in the long run.

That is what we lacked during the war. That is where our enemy was superior to us. We must make up for that. We must take the techniques and dominance of the other side's opinion apparatus, which is all they really had, and fill it with the fire of the soul and the glow of new ideas.

Propaganda, too, has a system. It cannot be stopped and started whenever one wishes. In the long run, it can only be effective in the service of great ideals and far-seeing principles. And propaganda must be learned. It must be led only by those with a fine and sure instinct for the often changeable feelings of a people. They must be able to reach into the world of the broad masses and draw out their wishes and hopes. The effective propagandist must be a master of the art of speech, of writing, of journalism, of the poster, and of the leaflet. He must have the gift to use the major methods of influencing public opinion such as the press, film, and radio to serve his ideas and goals.

This is particularly necessary in a day when technology is advancing. Radio is already yesterday's invention, since television will probably soon arrive. On the one hand, successful propaganda must be a master of these methods of political opinion, but on the other hand, it may not grow stale in using them. It must find new ways and methods every day to reach success. The nature of propaganda remains the same, but the means provided by advancing technology are becoming ever broader and far-reaching. One need only consider the revolutionary impact of the invention of radio, which gave the spoken word true mass effectiveness. The technology of propaganda has changed greatly in recent years, but the art of propaganda has remained the same.

Understood in this sense, propaganda has long since lost its odium of inferiority inherited from the past. It holds first rank among the arts with which one leads a nation. It is indispensable in building a modern state. It is something of a connecting link between government and people.

All propaganda has a bias. The quality of this bias determines whether propaganda has a positive or negative effect. Good propaganda does not need to lie; indeed, it may not lie. It has no reason to fear the truth. It is a mistake to believe that the people cannot take the truth. It can. It is only a matter of presenting the truth to the people in a way that it will be able to understand. A propaganda that lies proves that it has a bad cause. It cannot be successful in the long run. A good propaganda will always come along that serves a good cause. But propaganda is still necessary if a good cause is to succeed. A good idea does not win simply because it is good. It must be presented properly if it is to win. The combination makes for the best propaganda. Such propaganda is successful without being obnoxious. It depends on its nature, not its methods. It works without being noticed. Its goals are inherent in its nature. Since it is almost invisible, it is effective and powerful. A good cause will lose to a bad one if it depends only on its rightness, while the other side uses the methods of influencing the masses. We are, for example, firmly convinced that we fought the war for a good cause, but that was not enough. The world should also have known and seen that our cause was good. However, we lacked the effective means of mass propaganda to make that clear to the world. Marxism certainly did not fight for great ideals. Despite that, in November 1918 it overcame Kaiser, Reich, and the army because it was superior in the art of mass propaganda.

National Socialism learned from these two examples. It drew the correct practical conclusions from that knowledge. The ideal of a socialist national community did not remain mere theory with us, but became living reality in the thoughts and feelings of sixty-seven million Germans. Our propaganda of word and deed created the conditions for that. Mastering it kept National Socialism from the danger of remaining the dream and longing of a few thousand. Through propaganda, it became hard, steely everyday reality.

That which we only imperfectly and inadequately understood during the war became a virtuously mastered art during the rise of the National Socialist movement. Today one can say without exaggeration that Germany is a model of propaganda for the entire world. We have made up for past failures and developed the art of mass influence to a degree that puts the efforts of other nations into the shadows. The importance the National Socialist leadership placed on propaganda became clear when it established a Ministry for Public Education and Propaganda shortly after it took power. This ministry is entirely within the spirit of National Socialism, and comes from it. It unites what we learned as an opposition movement confronting the enemy and under persecution from an enemy system, sometimes more from necessity than desire. Recently some have tried to imitate this ministry and its concentration of all means of influencing opinion, but here, too, the slogan applies: "Often copied, never equaled."

The organizational union of mass demonstrations, the press, film, radio, literature, theater, and so forth, is only the mechanical side to the matter. It is not so much that all these means are in one hand. The important thing is that this hand knows how to master and control them. Establishing a central office is not difficult. What is difficult is finding people who are experts in an area previously not a concern of the state.

We could not have done that ourselves had we not been through the great school of our party. It was our teacher. During fourteen

JOSEPH GOEBBELS

years of opposition we gathered an enormous amount of knowledge, experience, wisdom, and ability. This made us able to use the wide-reaching methods of government propaganda without running the risk of losing the spirit behind them. Effective propaganda avoids any form of bureaucracy. It requires lightning-fast decisions, alert creativity, and inexhaustible inventiveness. The machinery of the organization would remain lifeless and rigid were it not constantly driven by the motor of the spirit and the idea.

It is, therefore, wrong to think that a ministry could replace what the movement alone is able to do. Cooperation between the party and the government was necessary for the major successes that we are proud of. Only when all means of propaganda are concentrated and their unified application assured is it possible to carry out major educational and propaganda battles, as we did before 12 November 1933 or 19 August 1934, which were of true historic significance.[2]

If such an art of active mass influence through propaganda is joined with the long-term systematic education of a nation, and if both are conducted in a unified and precise way, the relationship between the leadership and the nation will always remain close. From authority and following will develop that type of modern democracy for which Germany is the model for the entire world in the twentieth century.

That is also the basic requirement for any practical political activity. A government that wishes to be successful over the long term cannot ignore it. Its projects and plans would fail were they not supported by the people. But the people must understand them in order to accomplish them.

One can only smile when one looks over our borders at the efforts of parliamentary-democratic parties that are all worried about this. Their attitude seems to be: "How can I explain it to my child?" A fear of the people is the characteristic of liberal government theory. It has set the people free, and now does not know what to do with it. The hunt for popularity usually leads to nothing other than concealing the truth and speaking nonsense. One dares not say what is right, and what one does say leads to disaster. But that is presumably what the people wants. One no longer has the courage to say unpopular things, much less do them. The result is that major European problems are lost in useless debates while political, economic, and social crises of unprecedented magnitude face the nations.

There are times when statesmen must have the courage to do something unpopular. But their unpopular actions must be properly prepared, and must be put in the proper form, so that their peoples will understand. The man on the street is usually not as unreasonable as some think. Since it is he who usually has to bear the heaviest burdens that result from unpopular policies, he at least has a right to know why things are being done this way and not that way. All practical politics depends on how persuasive it is to the people. It is no sign of wise leadership to acquaint the nation with hard facts overnight. Crises must be prepared for not only politically and economically, but also psychologically. Here propaganda has its place. It must prepare the way actively and educationally. Its task is to prepare the way for practical actions. It must accompany these actions step by step, never losing sight of them. In a manner of speaking, it provides the background music. Such propaganda in the end miraculously makes the unpopular popular, enabling even a government's most difficult decisions to secure the resolute support of a people. A government that uses it properly can do what is necessary without running the risk of losing the masses.

Propaganda is therefore a necessary life function of the modern state. Without it, seeking great goals is simply impossible in this century of the masses. It stands at the beginning of practical political activity in every area of public life. It is its important and necessary prerequisite.

Let me give several recent examples. I need only sketch the details. They are too fresh in our memories to require elaboration.

There are no parliamentary parties in Germany any longer. How could we have overcome them had we not waged an educational campaign for years that persuaded the people of their weaknesses, harms, and disadvantages? Their final elimination was only the result of what the people had already realized. Our propaganda weakened these parties. Based on that, they could be eliminated by a legal act.

Marxism could not be eliminated by a government decision. Its elimination was the end result of a process that began with the people. But that was only possible because our propaganda had shown the people that Marxism was a danger to both the state and society. The positive national discipline of the German press would never have been possible without the complete elimination of the influence of the liberal-Jewish press. That happened only because of the years-long work of our propaganda. Today, particularism in Germany is something of the past. The fact that it was eliminated by a strong central idea of the Reich is no accident, but rather it depended on psychological foundations that were established by our propaganda.

Or consider economic policy. Does anyone believe that the idea of class struggle could have been eliminated by a law? Is it not rather the fact that the seeds we sowed in a hundred thousand meetings resulted in a new socialist structure of labor? Today employers and workers stand together in the Labor Front. The Law on National Labor is the foundation of our economic thinking, realizing itself more and more. Are not these social achievements the result of long and tireless labor by thousands of speakers?

Germany suffers from a shortage of foreign currency. This affects the people in serious ways. Propaganda once again is the key to dealing with the problem.

The Hereditary Farming Law, the idea of the Reich Agricultural Estate, market regulations in agriculture, all these need propaganda to show the people their importance, which is necessary if they are to succeed.

We could eliminate the Jewish danger in our culture because the people had recognized it as the result of our propaganda. Major cultural achievements such as the unique "Kraft durch Freude"[3] are possible only with the powerful support of the people. The prerequisite was and is propaganda, which here, too, creates and maintains the connection to the people.

The Winter Relief last year raised about 350 million marks. This was not the result of taxation, but rather many gifts of every amount. Everyone gave freely and gladly, many of whom in the past had done nothing in the face of similar need. Why?

Because a broad propaganda, using every modern means, presented the whole nation with the need for this program of social assistance.

Forty-five million Reich marks of goods and services were provided. Eighty-five million Reich marks worth of fuel were distributed. One hundred and thirty million Reich marks worth of food were given out. Ten million Reich marks worth of meals were provided, and seventy million Reich marks worth of clothing.

Some of these achievements were the result of donations in kind, others of cash contributions. Street collections, donations of a part of paychecks, contributions from companies, and gifts subtracted from bank accounts resulted in cash totaling 184 million Reich marks. Twenty-four million marks alone were the result of "One Pot Sundays."[4] The Reich itself added fifteen million marks to the contributions of the people. The railway system provided reduced or free shipping with a value of fourteen million marks.

Of our population of 65,595,000, 16,511,000 were assisted by the Winter Relief. There were 150,000 volunteers. There were only 4,474 paid workers, of whom 4,144 were in the thirty-four regional party offices, and 230 at the national headquarters.

Propaganda and education prepared the way for the largest social assistance program in history. They were the foundation. Their success was that, over a long winter, no one in Germany went hungry or was cold.

Over forty million people approved of the Führer's decision to leave the League of Nations on 12 November 1933. That gave him the ability to speak to the world in the name of the nation, defending honor, peace, and equality as the national ideals of the whole German people. The issues of disarmament were put on firm and clear foundations. Once again, propaganda was the foundation for the nation's unity on 12 November, and therefore of the freedom of action that the Führer had in foreign affairs.

Each situation brings new challenges. And each task requires the support of the people, which can only be gained by untiring propaganda that brings the broad masses knowledge and clarity. No area of public life can do without it. It is the never resting force behind public opinion. It must maintain an unbroken relationship between leadership and people. Every means of technology

JOSEPH GOEBBELS

must be put in its service; the goal is to form the mass will and to give it meaning, purpose, and goals that will enable us to learn from past failures and mistakes and ensure that the lead National Socialist strength has given us over other nations will never again be lost.

May the bright flame of our enthusiasm never fade. It alone gives light and warmth to the creative art of modern political propaganda. Its roots are in the people. The movement gives it direction and drive. The state can only provide it with the new, wide-ranging technical means. Only a living relationship between people, movement, and state can guarantee that the creative art of propaganda, of which we have made ourselves the world's master, will never sink into bureaucracy and bureaucratic narrow-mindedness.

Creative people made propaganda and put it in the service of our movement. We must have creative people who can use the means of the state in its service.

It is also a function of the modern state. It is the firm ground on which the state must stand. It rises from the depths of the people, and must always return to the people to find its roots and strength. It may be good to have power based on weapons. It is better and longer lasting, however, to win and hold the heart of a people.

NOTES

1. The source is *Der Kongreß zu Nürnberg vom 5. bis 10. September 1934. Offizieller Bericht über den Verlauf des Reichsparteitages mit sämtlichen Reden* (Munich: Franz Eher, 1934), 130–42.

2. The dates of two nationwide referendums that Hitler called.

3. The Nazi organization that provided recreational activities for workers.

4. One Sunday each month, people were encouraged to have a simple meal at home, donating the money saved to the Nazi charity.

Gertrud Scholtz-Klink

Duties and Tasks of the Woman
in the National Socialist State

OCTOBER 1936

National Socialism was a male-dominated movement. Hitler and the Nazis saw a woman's highest duty as bearing children, and the more the better. They instituted a medal for mothers who had given birth to at least four children. Politics and the professions were male preserves. Although the Nazis did not prohibit women from holding jobs before World War II began, they made it clear that women had better things to do than seek success in the male arena.

That did not mean the Nazis ignored women. In fact, as in every other area of life, they developed mass organizations to propagandize women. The most prominent leader in these organizations was Gertrud Scholtz-Klink (1902–1999). Blond, trim, and blue-eyed, she married at eighteen and had six children with her first husband, two of whom died. A second marriage ended in divorce. She married a third husband with six children from a previous marriage, and had another child with him. She practiced what she preached.

As "National Women's Leader" *(Reichsfrauenführer),* she headed the National Socialist Women's League, which had a membership in the millions. She also directed the national coalition of women's organizations, the women's section of the German Labor Front (the Nazi labor organization), and the women's division of the Red Cross.

A capable speaker, she was the only woman who regularly

spoke at the annual Nuremberg party rally, at which there was a mass meeting for women. She gave many other speeches as well. An analysis of her speeches concludes that she generally made arguments that were relevant and persuasive for her largely female audience.[1] In this speech, delivered to a large Nazi rally in 1936, and widely distributed in a pamphlet for several years thereafter, she makes clear what Nazism expected of German women. Women, she explains, are responsible for the home. If there are food shortages, the task of the male leadership is to look for large-scale solutions, whereas women are to be frugal and conserve the food that is available. Women, furthermore, are to be cheerful and supportive, setting an example of optimism.

She also takes up religion. The vast majority of the German population was at least nominally Christian. The Nazi Party in general, and Scholtz-Klink in particular, saw Christianity as a threat to the call for the total allegiance of the German population to Nazism's quasi-religious worldview. However, Nazism also knew that changing religious commitments took long years, and that directly attacking Christianity would be counterproductive. In this speech, therefore, Scholtz-Klink promotes a vague "positive Christianity" that led Christians who did not think too much about her words to overlook Nazism's real nature.

An unrepentant Nazi, Scholtz-Klink published a book thirty years after the end of World War II that maintained Nazi policies had been good for women.[2]

SPEECH DELIVERED TO A PARTY RALLY, 1936

The great event of which we are all today a part is the growth of a new German people's order, a people's order at the center of which stands the great thought and compelling idea of the people's community.[3] This compelling central idea for all of us, the people's community, obliges not only the individual, but also organizations, institutions, schools, and clubs, to consider themselves and their activities from this standpoint. It has proven necessary for some of us, and some organizations in our state, to renew themselves, to relearn and rethink, and this rethinking has carried us all along, such that nothing really has remained unaffected. Everything that we do in Germany to capture and educate the German people, both individually and in relationship to the community, must follow new laws.

Our evening together is intended to set a direction, a path, for our work, to be a self-analysis. I wish to begin by asking ourselves a question. How did people treat us in the past, as we were growing into a community, and how must we treat our people today? All of us in this hall began as little pioneers of the Führer with a special task, and all of you who are here today, both men and women, know that the German people today needs those who understand the history of their people, and the relationships within the people, in order for them to use this knowledge of the development of their people to see clearly new paths.

I wish to begin my discussion of yesterday and today at the most basic level, when one for the first time places a person in a community, bringing him into a particular relationship with the people. It is the first time in which a person is forced to give up egotistic thinking and come to terms with his environment: in school. It is each person's first step in joining the community, that first bitter step that forces him to face the problems of life, even if it is only learning his ABCs. I said before that our people needs those who know the history of their people, the relationships, the where from and why of intellectual events, and who understand a spiritual mission. If we look back ten, fifteen years—no, even more, twenty or twenty-five years—all those here who had the good fortune to attend secondary schools will have to agree with me that we learned little about the history of our people and its spiritual mission at that time. We often knew more about the history of the Romans, the Greeks, and above all the history of the Jewish people, than we did about German history. You surely know the Jewish prophets just as much by heart today as I do. We were taught about that much better, or at least more energetically, than we were taught the details of German history. And what we knew about German matters was so inadequate that we did not receive a year-by-year survey of a particular period in our history in each subject. We did not, in a given school year, get a good picture of a particular period of German history. Rather, to put it crudely, in the first hour in science class, we got something about the ice age. In the second hour, maybe something about the Minnesingers in literature, and in the third hour, some specialized bit of history. Our history teacher, for example, might tell us passionately and compellingly about the necessary and beneficial influence of the sun in Italy on political developments in Germany. Now, the spiritual outlook of this history teacher consisted of a happy mixture of absolute patriotism on the one hand, and—since he was a progressive man—an apostle of humanity on the other hand. That lovely phrase "national-liberal" applied to him, meaning "both the one thing and its opposite." We should not be surprised that, in the end, my dear fellow Germans, the first station of our childhood produced Germans who had mastered one-sided, limited knowledge from an objective standpoint, and had entirely forgotten and ignored the fact that there is also a subjective way of viewing the world, in which German people with German eyes and German hearts could have seen German things.

And that was no surprise. We had not learned the connections between things. At the next stage of education, we got even more of this limited training in life. We went to our universities, which centered on absolute specialization. In the individual subjects, as a result of this crazy training of specialists, the result was that the most specialized authorities fought about their particular "theory as such." The greatest pride of these scholars, I may say, was often to defend a "thing itself," never saying anything about how it would meet particular needs of the people, how it could serve and benefit the interests of the whole people. No, their greatest pride was in the "thing itself."

That is the education we grew up with; that is how we were educated in school. Then we were turned loose, and we were supposed to build a worldview and join the world. That was our life until the Führer came along. He grabbed us by our ears and said something like this: "My dear people, you really have to learn to go this way, thinking not of your own little self, of your wants and your specialty, but rather you have to see once more what your people's needs demand of you." In other words, the Führer taught us once again to see duty as the center of everything that we do.

He taught us that all labor, all knowledge, all learning, all battles, are not "things in themselves," but rather a holy task of each in service of the community of all. We had to follow this thinking to win our battles.

Each of us took this people's community as our duty, and we said: "Now, my dear friend, you may know a great deal about your field, and you may do wonderful things, but you have to understand something. Your knowledge alone, that we once made almost into an idol in Germany, has ruined your way of seeing the world." For the more I know, the more I realize how many things there are in the universe about which I know nothing. When I devote myself to a science, that lovely picture I have of the world is ruined. Only quietly growing wisdom leads me gradually to a deeper, greater understanding and experience of the connections things have with each other, and brings me to an understanding of an organic whole. We must learn to understand all of our individual things within the totality of our people, and to put them in service of our entire people. Getting back to the schools, that is why we mothers, based on our own school experiences, said: "Give German children a school that is free of all knowledge about foreign things and foreign countries—even though that has its place. From the first year of school on, give children a comprehensive view of things German so that children learn what we only learned later in life, thanks to the Führer: a respect for labor, and for the role of knowledge as the forerunner of wisdom."

The work of the National Socialist Women's League stood and stands under the influence of this process of renewal. It must first examine and review itself. What can we change, what can we do even better, and how can we once again learn a respect for labor as the source of and path to the wisdom we all need? And after that, how can we show this path to others through our manner, our words, our attitudes, our work? In the course of our efforts, we have the task of showing other women, millions of German women, how to be part of the process of moving from selfish "I" to the "you" of the people's community, to join our work and to win them over to National Socialism. That is why we have established the German Women's Work, which you are probably all familiar with, alongside the NS Women's League. We established the

Women's Office within the German Labor Front to deal with the particular socio-political problems of women—gaining respect for working women, protecting working mothers. Each office has its tasks. The most beautiful, the most noble thing about the whole work, however, is not that the Women's League is a particularly good political-worldview school, or that the Women's Office takes particularly good care of women in the socio-political arena, or that Home Assistance and the Mother's Service do their work. Rather, the most important thing is that we once again see ourselves as women who do their own work, but also share a single fanatic will to care once again for our people. Each who needs help knows that he can come at any time and find an understanding partner and comrade. I recently read a poem written by a woman worker. She wrote:

> My father goes to work in the foundry,
> Where he hammers iron into steel.
> I am proud of his strength,
> But he never laughs.
>
> My mother is an industrious woman,
> She works from dawn to dusk.
> And once—I know for sure—
> She smiled at me.

These words reveal the whole political history of our age. Man and woman perform hard, unending work, and both do their best. The man is sometimes hard, and sometimes too serious. He no longer laughs, and goes his way with determination. The woman stands beside him. She does her work using all her strength, as does he. But what she needs to do beyond that, my dear women, is the core of our work with women. What needs to be added here is what that girl said in her little poem: "Once she smiled at me." We women must bring something else to our work. We must not be nervous, but rather keep calm, and second, we must be ready at any time to give a cheerful smile for anyone who needs one. From this last thought, from this style of living, we will deal with all those things that could somehow hurt our people.

At the moment, for example, we talk a lot about meat short-ages. Most of the time, we talk too much about it. On the other hand, we talk a lot about job training. Someone may ask me: But what does the meat shortage have to do with job training, and job training with the housewife? Let me give you a real example. We know that sometimes we do not have enough of this or that kind of meat. On the other hand, we train restaurant employees, man-agers in the restaurant industry, housewives, and servants. Then we see all sorts of men and women in our cities who work outside their home, and hear them ask: Can you tell me a restaurant that does not always serve the same meat and sauces, but rather one where there are more potatoes, vegetables, salads, and so on? So we train restaurant employees to be the best cooks in the world.

What would happen if we combined the practical with the necessary in this area, and made part of the Reich occupation-al competition for women the making of wonderful food items with many vegetables, potatoes, and salads, but with less or even no meat? If the Führer says that we do not have enough foreign currency to import all the meat that we want, and that we have always imported in the past, then we housewives can prove our good education by simply saying: We have enough bread. We have enough potatoes. We have enough milk and sugar for the whole year. So let us set a table on which we serve potatoes for the evening meal along with other pleasant things that we have gathered by good household management, such as red cabbage, radish salad, celery salad, and all those other lovely simple things. One does not always have to have meat sandwiches for dinner, as is the case in so many households. In millions of homes, we will, for a while, prepare more healthy potatoes, leaving the meat for those who need it because they are heavy laborers. First of all, it will not hurt those people who work with their minds, or who do light physical labor, if they eat a little less meat. It will even help their waistline. And second, is it not more than right that people who are brothers and sisters, who have the same mother, namely Germany, support and help each other? That is how things are in any decent family, and that is how we want to behave. I tell you this only to help you see that today, in the last analysis, the Ger-man housewife is really the best minister of economics, since if we women would only work together systematically toward this goal, the Führer and his whole economic staff would not have to work nearly as hard.

I must say something more. We have given back honor to the housewife, which she had lost during the Marxist era. You all remember the time when people said: "I would really rather have a job. It is nice to be a housewife, to be taken care of, but it is 'unproductive labor'—a phrase that was tossed around so much in Germany. "As a stenographer I can see at the end of the day what I have accomplished, but one sees nothing of a housewife's 'unproductive labor,' unless one perhaps counts the ever fatter belly of her husband as 'productive labor.' But that is hardly enough satisfaction for one's life. To the contrary, over time it can become a burden." This phrase about the "unproductive labor" of women brought the work of the housewife into disrepute, even though it is one of the most economically important factors in a nation. Such a phrase could only develop in an age that understood productivity only as that which went into one's own pocket, that visibly flowed to one's own family, something one could count, touch, but never anything that served the whole people, and therefore indirectly each individual as well.

Let me give you a small example of just how productive the housewife is. If each of the 17 1/2 million families in Germany carelessly throws away one slice of bread that weighs fifty grams each week—that is only a small slice of bread—, that means 8,750 quintals of bread per month (sic), or 445,000 quintals a year. That is 4,000 railway cars full of bread. Now, ladies, think of how often a piece of bread is carelessly left uneaten. When one comes across excursionists on a Sunday afternoon, one sees bread carelessly left on the ground and literally stepped on. Think of the exhausting labor the Führer expends to win land from the sea, meter by meter, and now calculate how much land would be necessary to harvest 450,000 quintals of grain. We are thus stomping on ground that we do not have, but bitterly need, without thinking anything at all about it. You may say to me that some of those 17 1/2 million households are rural households, and they do not waste anything. Women, I know that a farming woman does not waste any bread because she has greater respect for the earth than someone who lives in a city. But if even half of this bread is wasted and ends up in city trash cans or somewhere else, we have shown that we badly need to learn what our forefathers knew: a respect for the earth and for its gifts. We must once again learn this respect. We must say to the women in the city: "Just as your asphalt streets have covered the earth, as the earth gradually vanished beneath them, so, too, has the asphalt in your hearts covered up your respect for the earth and your knowledge of your dependence on that earth."

We certainly do not want to say that we should tear up the asphalt and go back to nature. We do want to hammer something else into their hearts: "City man and city woman, do not forget that under your asphalt is the earth that you must be thankful for the fact that you can live and work on asphalt streets." That is what we must tell city-dwellers. That will gradually lead people back to a respect for the earth and its gifts. That leads us to something else. In late fall comes the harvest. The earth provides us well and generously, but it does not spoil us. We must therefore take good care of the harvest and lay up stores for the time when the earth needs rest and cannot give us any gifts. Otherwise, we ask for fresh vegetables and things in January that the earth can no longer provide, and complain when what we want is too expensive, because it does not come from our own earth. At our thanksgiving festival, we must therefore enjoy the gifts that nature gives us, so that we will be able to get through the times when she can give us nothing, and when the Führer needs the money we formerly used for too many imports for things he considers more important at the moment. I believe we can be sure that the Führer asks nothing of us, and thinks nothing necessary, unless he can really justify it to himself and to the nation.

German women! That is but one practical side of our work. We must talk about it with each other constantly. As we work with mothers in public health through our Mother's Service, we must also make clear to mothers that our children are the most valuable possession we have, second only to our honor. We must understand their development, and how to care for them before we get married. These are all ways of building bridges to each other. The Mother's Service is another bridge, as are home economics and all the other areas, such as the Red Cross or caring for working women. All our work is a bridge on which we must find the way to each other, from which we really must look into the hearts of others and say: "Do you not want to work with us? It is pleasant, and we need one another, for today we are responsible for each other." The Führer has given us responsibility for the entire German people.

You may say to me: "Sure, but listen to me. I cannot be responsible for every person who lives in my neighborhood. Each person has his own nature, his own character, his own attitudes. I cannot be responsible for them." Men and women! We probably cannot be responsible for a person's nature or his basic character, but we are responsible for the influence we have had on his life and his path, that is, whether we have pulled him down or helped him to rise. We are responsible for our part of him. How else can a community justify itself before life and before God if it is not responsible for the attitude that it shows to others? I know that that is terribly difficult. It is difficult because we have to always see that the courage to do good we have within ourselves is stronger than our fear of the evil in the world. We must also work to see that our courage to draw on our own strength, our own devotion, to help others is somewhat stronger than the all too human tendency to inertia and comfort. These are the two things we must do. Often when we say to someone that you are responsible for someone else, that you are responsible for your attitude toward him, he replies: "Leave me alone. I have enough to do already. I have to worry about myself and cannot do it for someone else. I have not done so before. Leave me alone." People by nature are inclined to inertia when it comes to making demands on themselves, to struggling with themselves. We must shed this inertia because we are part of a community and because we call ourselves comrades.

What does the word "comrade" mean? The word is used today very, very often as a slogan. Everyone says "comrade" to everyone else. He does not think about what that means. One thinks that "comrade" means that you and I have the same job. Another thinks that "comrade" means that if I do something stupid or do something wrong, you will not say anything about it. You can behave badly next time, and I will not say anything about it either. Each thinks that a "comrade" will cover his own failings if necessary. I believe that we can only call those people comrades, and we may only ask for camaraderie, if we realize that the nature of camaraderie is that I can be the biggest enemy of my comrade when necessary if I notice that he is doing things from spiritual laziness that are hurting him. Then I must go to him and say: "My dear friend, I cannot support you in this. You are taking things so easy that you are not using your strength and gifts, but rather are being lazy and comfortable. If I am really to be your comrade, my duty is to show you what you could be if you only put forth a little effort." That is camaraderie, for true camaraderie sees not the moment, but rather looks at others and says: "There is something greater than you or me, that stands above you and me." That is the community in which we live and in which we find ourselves not by accident, for centuries of labor by the best German fathers and mothers raised us and supported us. Since we see this, comrades are those people who honor the greatest and the strongest that is within people, and who have the drive to draw out the best and most beautiful from others.

I wanted to say that, women, because we often speak of our camaraderie, it is important that we know how beautiful and strong it is. We are building a chain through our camaraderie, and take each others' hands. It may be that one or another sometimes tires or loses courage, that he complains or causes trouble—that is part of life—but what he may not do and what cannot happen, is that he collapses during these weary hours, lacking courage. We must be surrounded by a circle so strong that each can confidently depend upon it. We then say to him: "My dear friend, you are tired today. You have a problem that we cannot at the moment help with, because there are things that one cannot take from other people. This we can do. We can lend you our strength, our community, our loyalty, and if need be our tears, until the day comes when you can laugh and be happy again."

We have good reason to do that, since we Germans are cheerful people. I know that we are so often misunderstood. People say to me: "You always preach that people should be cheerful. You are cheerful yourself, but we have no job, or only part-time work, not enough income." Do you think, my dear lady, that I do not know that? I know how hard it is to feed a batch of children with only a few marks. I also know, however, that we will never make our people National Socialists, even with all the money and all the lovely things and all our work, if we do not first persuade people to take a cheerful and confident attitude toward life.

Since I know that, we must begin where we can. Obviously, a person needs a job, an income, and that will happen as fast as possible. However, doing what we can in our community through our loyalty and our faith to make people cheerful can be done at any time. We can start immediately, and make a beginning. That is why we women have made that beginning.

Another thing on cheerfulness. We would be the most thankless of people if we were not cheerful people, despite all our difficulties. Let me tell you about an experience I had a few days ago with a person after a meeting. He said to me: "You preach to people about joy and strength and love." I had spoken about these things during the meeting, and mentioned that when we think of what God gives the Führer, what he gives each of us, in terms of physical and spiritual strengths, we have to say that that alone is never-ending proof of the love and blessings of God, for which we should be cheerful and thankful. "Well," the man said, "the God that you and the other Nazis preach to people is the God of love. That is simple enough. But what about the other God, who punishes and torments? You do not have anything to say about that." I replied: "My dear friend, I must ask you something. Have you ever experienced love yourself, indeed, love for another person?" He looked at me in puzzlement for a moment and said: "Sure, of course." I then said to him: "No one with even a spark of goodness in him can escape the impact of great and noble human love. He will always try, somehow, without even thinking about it, to be worthy of that love. He will be thankful and cheerful. He will want to be good, and if he sins against this love only in the slightest, he will be ashamed—you know this. It is not necessary that someone else preach him a long sermon to show him that he has sinned against love. If in my limited human nature I can express such love, and have such great effect on a person, well, how much more powerful must be the strength of the love of God, and its impact on people!" When I see how, every day and every hour, our work blesses many thousands of people, I sense the vast love of God. Why should I not take my fellow people and comrades by the hand and say: "Be cheerful and see God's great love in the world." Why should I say to them: "But watch out! One day, God will be angry with you"? If we who sense God's love sin against the love of God through a deed, a thought, or an action, we should not consider even the simplest person in Germany so base as not to be at least as ashamed before God as he would before a person whose love he had sinned against.

We believe that one makes people stronger and brings them farther with positive rather than with negative things. We do not want a German to think so little of the Lord God that he needs him only when he has done something bad, that God almost has to appear to him in person and to say: "You have done something bad." We want people once more to be ashamed themselves, but not to grovel, but rather to say: "Dear God, I was a foolish, weak person, but I will see to it that I make up for it ten times before I come to you again."

Women and men! The work we do, be it economic-social, social-political, or whatever it may be, is only a path to this final personal knowledge, to this final affirmation of the tasks life has given us. We National Socialists have already had to learn a great deal, and we may still have more to learn during these difficult times, to remind ourselves of, and to pass on, our faith in the greatness and immensity of God, of this love that we sense. We have to do this for one simple reason. Today, unfortunately, we encounter some people who hold an office and think themselves God's representative. But instead of transmitting that love as a source of strength, they often come across more as the strict agent of God than as his humble agent. We want to make the love of God part of the experience of the people we encounter. As we continued our conversation, the man I mentioned earlier said to me: "You are fighting for Christ's teaching. Do you at least believe in Christ?" I thought for a moment, and replied: "I can only give you my personal answer. I believe that it is much more important for us to ask our German people: 'Dear German, will you try to believe in the way Christ believed, and from this strength live a life as true and as strong as the life he lived? He gave us probably the truest, most brotherly and strongest example of a life that has ever been lived in this world.'"

Therefore, women, if we are asked "Do you believe in Christ?" we can answer calmly: "I will try to believe as he believed, with that great strength and selflessness." If we have understood that, we will no longer ask: "Are you Catholic or Protestant, or whatever?" We will then know that once we have believed as Christ believed, we will live in an honest, strong, loyal, and cooperative way. Our life will be an affirmation of his work and his attitude and his loyalty toward our neighbor. Then, perhaps, we will be able to say: "God is so immeasurably great and incomprehensible that it is presumptuous of humans to fight about Him."

Believe me, women, in our meetings we must, more than ever before, say: "We first of all want to become people with much more respect for the language of a powerful life, and thereby as well people who have respect for God and for their fellow men, who are a small atom of God.

"Second, as people who have learned such respect, we want to spread this experience to our comrades, to give them strength. And as people and comrades, we want to become ever better Germans, who give their mortal lives in the service of our great age, so that the Führer can create an eternal Germany from our obedience."

Notes

1. Massimiliano Livi, *Gertrud Scholtz-Klink: Politische Handlungsräume und Identitätsprobleme der Frauen im Nationalsozialismus am Beispiel der "Führerin aller deutschen Frauen"* (Münster, Germany: Lit Verlag, 2005), 129.
2. Gertrud Scholtz-Klink, *Die Frau im Dritten Reich. Eine Dokumentation* (Tübingen, Germany: Grabert, 1978).
3. The source is Gertrud Scholtz-Klink, *Verpflichtung und Aufgabe der Frau im nationalsozialistischen Staat. Eine Rede der Reichsfrauenführerin auf der Frauenkundgebung anläßlich des Kreisparteitages der NSDAP. in München, Oktober 1936* (Berlin: Junker und Dünnhaupt Verlag, 1939).

Gerhard Wagner

Race and Population Policy

11 SEPTEMBER 1936

Gerhard Wagner (1888–1938), a physician, was head of the National Socialist German Physicians' Association and also held other important positions. He gave speeches at the annual Nuremberg rallies that outlined Nazi racial and medical views. The Nuremberg rallies not only had huge audiences at the scene, but also were reprinted in most newspapers, and republished in large editions in books and pamphlets. This, then, is a speech that nearly every German had a chance to read, even if many probably preferred to avoid reading a long speech with familiar material.

Wagner was a vehement anti-Semite, and this speech has strong anti-Semitic elements, but most of it emphasizes the other side of Nazi racial policy. The Nazis viewed Jews as racially inferior, but they also thought it necessary to take active measures to improve the racial quality of the "Aryan" population.[1] Wagner outlines Nazi plans to resolve three issues.

First, the purity of the German race will be guaranteed by prohibiting intermarriage between Jews and Germans. At the 1935 Nuremberg rally, Hitler had proclaimed racial laws that banned intermarriage. The problem the Nazis faced was definitional. How much "Jewish blood" did it take to be a Jew? A complicated series of regulations allowed quarter Jews to marry full "Aryans," which distressed some Nazis who thought that those with any Jewish ancestry should not be permitted to marry "Aryans." Wagner assures such doubters that the German population will safely absorb the limited number of quarter Jews.

Second, Wagner discusses "life unworthy of life," those with physical and mental defects who he argues are a costly burden on the state. Money that should go to support the healthy instead preserves worthless lives. Consistent with Nazi policy, he discusses sterilizing those with mental or physical deficiencies. Such rhetoric laid the foundation for the subsequent Nazi euthanasia campaign.

Third, he discusses measures the state will take to support healthy children, and to increase the German birthrate. This, too, was a critical topic. Before the Nazis took power, the German birthrate had been declining, and there were forecasts of the same kind of demographic decline that Europeans are speaking of today. The Nazis promptly introduced a range of measures to encourage Germans to marry and have children, and with considerable success.

One should recall that ideas of eugenics were widely shared during the 1930s. In the United States, thousands were involuntarily sterilized in an effort to improve the quality of the population. As Wagner notes, many throughout the world were attracted by the prospect of improving the human genetic stock. It is, therefore, not surprising that the eugenics ideal of a pure and healthy race was attractive to many Germans. It was the "sunny side" of Nazi racial policy. Who could be against policies that promoted healthy children?

SPEECH DELIVERED AT THE NUREMBERG RALLY, 11 SEPTEMBER 1936

What the world has been most interested in is the program, policies, and actions of National Socialism that have to do with its new approach to the concepts of race and population policy.[2]

From my experience, one can divide those who still respond to the new Germany's measures in these regards with a lack of understanding, uncertainty, opposition, or even hostility, into several groups.

One group consists of émigrés and ignoramuses. I group them together because we are going to ignore them. Even the gods fight in vain against ignorance and stupidity, and émigré lies have become so outrageous and tasteless that they find ever fewer gullible listeners abroad.

Another group consists of scholars and scientists, a group steadily becoming smaller, even abroad, as is clear from the most varied decisions of foreign and international scientific societies that agree with our racial hygiene measures and our genetic policies. We can only say to these learned critics that our genetic and racial thinking stems in the end not from our scientific, but rather from our National Socialist convictions, and that it was not learned scientists, but rather our Führer Adolf Hitler, and he alone, who made genetic and racial thinking the center of our National Socialist worldview and the foundation of the rebuilding of our people's state. The doctrines of blood and race are not primarily an important and interesting piece of biological science to us, but rather above all else a political-ideological attitude that fundamentally determines our attitudes toward all matters and questions of life.

More important than these two groups to us, however, are those who reject or oppose us because they hold to another worldview.

Those who base their materialist image of the world on the doctrines of a liberal or Marxist era cannot understand how we can have dethroned their idols of "the economy and Mammon," replacing them at the center of our National Socialist process of construction and renewal with the German man, with the German people.

The other groups with a worldview warn their sheep in Christian piety, and in the name of both confessions, of the errors of National Socialist genetic and racial doctrines, and of the errors of the measures taken by the Third Reich. I have this request to those who, in contrast to the communist and Marxist foreign apostles, overtly and covertly go about their business at home: When you don the worthy priestly robes of either confession and claim that "your kingdom is not of this world," please concern yourselves with your kingdom and leave to us the responsibility for the kingdom of this world. Allow us to form our German state according to our laws and needs.

My fellow party members, you know the reasons for our National Socialist population and racial policies. We want to rescue a dying people from the edge of the abyss and bring it back to the paths that will lead, according to human reason, to a future in the coming millennium. We must oppose the three great dangers of racial and biological decline that have repeatedly destroyed states, peoples, and cultures in the past if they did not succeed in resisting them in good time. We must therefore contend with three issues: the decline in the birthrate, the increase in sick and unfit genes in our people, and the mixing of the blood of our people with that of foreign and unrelated peoples, in particular with Jewish blood.

When I spoke here a year ago about the necessity of a law to protect German blood, none of us imagined that a few days later the Führer would present his people with the bold Nuremberg Laws, the "Reich Citizenship Law" and the "Law for the Protection of German Blood and German Honor." The law to protect German blood created clarity in the Jewish Question, and the Reich citizenship law fulfilled points 4 and 5 of the National Socialist program.

Points 4 and 5 state:

> "Only racial comrades may be citizens. A racial comrade can only be someone of German blood, without regard to religious confession. No Jew can therefore be a citizen."
> "He who is not a citizen may live in Germany only as a guest, and must abide by the laws for foreigners."

The Nuremberg Laws replaced the concept of "citizen of the state" with "citizen of the Reich." That by itself had only formal significance. It did not by itself realize the demands of the party program.

However, the Nuremberg Laws make further infiltration of Jewish blood into the German national body impossible. To National Socialists, whose racial standpoint is anchored in blood, the broad scope of this historic decision makes all other political and economic aspects of laws regarding the Jews of secondary importance.

The Nuremberg Laws would have been incomplete and unfinished had they not dealt with the status of the so-called German-

Jewish half-breeds, that is, half and quarter Jews. This bastard-ized mixed race is not wanted, and the goal of the legislation is to make it disappear—both biologically and politically—as soon as possible. The marriage regulations will lead to that. A quarter Jew may only marry someone of full German blood, and a half Jew, provided he has not chosen to belong to the Jewish religion, or as we prefer, married a Jewish partner and thereby joined the Jewish people, may marry a German only with the permission of the Ministry of the Interior and the Deputy Führer.

It came as no surprise to us, indeed it was what we expected, that the Nuremberg Laws were a welcome occasion for World Jewry and their allies to scream about the "German barbarians." It is not worth the time to look into all these varied complaints. Our handling of the Jewish question is a matter of domestic German policy, but we do hope that many of our foreign Olympic guests were able to see for themselves how badly things are going for the "poor Jews" in terrible Nazi Germany.

To those who think that our regulations on the marriage of half Jews in Germany are unreasonable—or depending on their attitudes, inhumane or unchristian—I can only say that if the church can demand celibacy of hundreds of thousands, we believe before our God and our consciences that it is good and beneficial for our German people to implement marriage regulations for 200,000 half Jews.

I can well understand those German racial comrades who want to refuse any mixture of foreign Jewish blood at all, and who cannot understand why the marriage regulations of the Nuremberg Laws permit marriage to quarter Jews. To them I say that there are practical and political reasons for the marriage regulations, and that we have confidence that our sixty-seven million people will be able to absorb the blood of 100,000 quarter Jews—there are no more than that—without significant damage.

But those who believe that the Jewish question has been fully settled and resolved in Germany by the Nuremberg Laws must know that the battle goes on. World Jewry itself is seeing to that. We will be victorious only when each German racial comrade knows that it is a matter of our very existence. The party's educational and training work seems to me more necessary than ever before, since even some party comrades see these matters as no longer relevant or important.

People are always saying that our National Socialist racial thinking is materialistic, unchristian, chauvinistic, imperialistic, and that it leads to the defamation of foreign races and peoples. The opposite is the case. We believe that our racial policy is the surest guarantee for mutual respect and for peaceful coexistence between the peoples of this world. Someone of another race is different from me both in body and soul, for both are important. This makes no value judgment about other races. We are too conscious of the relationship between our own blood and our own race to presume to make such a judgment, which could only come from a standpoint that thought itself above race and humanity.

Scientifically, differences between races and peoples are incontrovertible. That is the foundation, the justification, and also the obligation of any racial policy, without which, according to our view, Europe and the whole world can never be at peace. The National Socialist state would never use military action to forcibly take over nations or populations that differ from us in blood and soul, since they would forever remain foreign elements within our state. We therefore reject chauvinism and imperialism, since we grant to other races on this earth the same right we claim for ourselves, namely the right to form our own life and environment according to the necessities and laws of our nature. Racial policy is thus to us a policy of peace.

Finally, a word to those who reject our racial policy as "unchristian." God has chosen to create humanity in the form of various races, as he has done in all of the rest of nature. Those who ignore race and its laws are not acting in a Christian manner, but rather we claim to be following the will of God, who has created the various racial types of this world so that each may maintain the greatest possible racial purity that will enable it to develop its particular strengths.

I turn next to the second process of biological decline that has long been evident in our people: an improper selection that has neglected the most valuable elements in an almost criminal manner, while providing for and supporting the inferior with endless resources.

The millions and billions that we have spent in the past, and the about one billion marks that we sacrifice today for the care of the genetically ill, is a waste of our national resources that we National Socialists cannot justify when we consider the needs of the healthy population. Healthy working class families with numerous children today earn only enough for the necessities of life, which means that it is irresponsible that the state must provide the money for some genetically ill families that may have several family members in institutions for years, costing thousands of marks annually.

The National Socialist state cannot repair the failings of the past, but through the "Law for the Prevention of Genetically Ill Offspring," it has seen to it that in the future the inferior will not be able to produce more inferior children, saving the German people from a steady stream of new genetic and economic burdens.

I discussed these matters in greater detail at the last two party rallies, so I will here respond only to several objections that have been made that might worry or concern innocent and gullible souls, though the objections are outbalanced by constantly growing praise from the whole world.

To those who claim that we act in an unchristian way, sinning against the will of God, we reply that we are convinced that we are acting consistently with the will of the creator when we prevent unhealthy life from being propagated, saving children and their children from new and enormous misery. The creator himself established the laws of life, which harshly and brutally let all that is unworthy of life perish to make room for the strong and healthy to whom the future belongs. This is necessary for the preservation and development of all that lives on this earth.

Even more absurd is the objection that our law on the sterilization of the genetically ill permits sterilization without their explicit consent. We think it would be ridiculous to allow the genetically ill, who may lack intelligence—as with the feeble-minded—or free will—as in the case of the mentally ill—to make decisions on the far more important matters of procreation and children, particularly since we already control their use of money and other lifeless things.

As for you critics from the communist-Marxist camp, we refuse you the right to judge whether we are acting correctly when we prevent inferior life as long as you promote the unlimited right to abortion when the growing life is valuable, whenever the mother, a doctor, or someone else wishes it.

I believe that we have a good conscience before the world when we eliminate life that is unworthy of life, particularly when we see everywhere that the poisonous seed of communism is senselessly slaughtering thousands of valuable people.

But the National Socialist state is interested in more than merely preventing the spread of unfit genes. Just as important, indeed even more important, are the measures that aim to care for and promote the nation's valuable genes.

The most important measure since the last party rally is the "Law for the Protection of the Genetic Health of the German People" of 18 October 1935. As a "healthy marriage act," it returns marriage to its real purpose—producing healthy children. It provides for careful marriage counseling to ensure that people will marry only if it can be expected that their children will be healthy—genetically healthy.

A large number of other measures promote health and physical ability, maintain the military and productive readiness of the German people, and advance these by all possible means.

The duty of the state is to protect the people's health through legal measures, and to ensure that these policies are implemented. The task of the movement is to win the support of the people for these government policies, and to reestablish the sense of responsibility individuals have toward themselves, their families, and their people. The rights and necessities of the whole people supersede the right of the individual to his own body.

The state is responsible for ensuring health; the party is responsible for providing leadership in the area. The two reinforce and support the same goal: the maintenance and improvement of the strength of the German people.

Successful leadership in the area of health is primarily in the hands of the approximately 20,000 expert physicians with a reliable worldview who are organized in the Office for Public Health. They are the foundation of the confidence that must exist between those who will lead and those who are to be led. We do not believe this confidence develops in the offices of state physicians, but rather only in personal contact between the individual citizen and a doctor whom he trusts. Our ideal, therefore, is not based on the laws, regulations, and rulings of experienced state doctors, but rather in the German people's doctor, the old family doctor, who respects nature and knows how to use its healing powers—which have often been criminally ignored in the past. Of course, he also understands the methods of academic medicine. Since he understands racial hygiene, he will never forget the people as a whole when he treats the individual. Prevention is more important to the doctor than healing! He wants to be a faithful aide not only in time of sickness, but also a counselor and a friend when someone is healthy. He is happier with a child who runs toward him with joy than with the most interesting and perhaps the most lucrative sickness.

I know that confidence in the German doctor suffered in many places in the past. I know that a comprehensive restructuring of a profession does not happen overnight, but rather requires a reasonable time. But I also know that an ever growing number of our German doctors are conscious of the great responsibility they have in the front lines of the battle for the strength and preservation of our people's blood, the most valuable treasure we possess, the one thing that—once lost—can never be regained.

History teaches us that in the long run peoples are not destroyed by economics or politics, by natural catastrophes, wars, or inner struggles, but rather the last and ultimate cause behind every people's decline throughout history has a biological cause that broke their strength and health. Many peoples have suffered heavy blows, including huge losses of living racial comrades, yet recovered within a few generations because their fertility was unharmed and their will to live remained healthy and strong. How often have healthy children sprung from the wombs of a defeated people and grown to become avengers and liberators who led their people to new greatness and to new triumphs.

Strength and health are given but once to a people, and once lost, they can never be regained, unlike destroyed cities and ruined fields.

In this regard, it is valuable to look at conditions in the Russian Soviet Union.

Although for understandable reasons it is not reported in official statistics and reports, various announcements and newspaper articles make it clear that health conditions in Russia are becoming more and more catastrophic.

Let me read you several reports from the Soviet press.

Communist Pravda writes on 24 February 1936: All the hospitals in Moscow were built over twenty or thirty years ago. No major repairs have been made for decades. The ceiling and walls of the department of infectious diseases were last painted in 1925. Hospitals are constantly short of needles, smocks, hand towels, as well as body and hand soap. In the leading Moscow model clinic, the bedding is tattered, and the mattresses, as in most hospitals, are entirely worn out.

Pravda of 7 July 1935 complains about criminal conduct against the health of workers and provides distressing numbers about illnesses resulting from unhealthy working conditions at the Moscow factory for measuring instruments during the first half of the year 1934.

It is also striking that, according to a report from Louis Fisher in the *Neuer Tagebuch* in 1936, the number of births in Moscow has steadily declined in recent years from 30.7 to 15.3 [per thousand], that is by more than half, and the number of abortions has increased by a factor of six. It is one and a half times as large as the number of births.

These reports make it clear that Russian leaders have allowed unbelievable damage to be done to their people's health that will have bitter consequences for this people and for its military strength. To these Russian communist leaders, their people are only puppets in the battle for power, be that a struggle between various Jewish cliques or the struggle to establish communist-Jewish world domination. The well-known Franciscan priest and sociologist Duffee, who is certainly not guilty of any great love for Germany, wrote in the *New York Times* of 14 July 1936 that he had come to the conclusion, after six years of research, that communism was only a facade for international capitalism.[3] We can only hope, in the interests of humanity, that this knowledge spreads more and more throughout the world.

My party comrades, we must understand that all the measures of our population policy that I have already described to you only make sense when the corresponding population is at hand, and the birthrate is sufficient to keep the population at the necessary level.

The German people grew from forty-two million to sixty-seven million between 1870 and today not through an increase in the birthrate, but only because the death rate steadily fell, resulting in an increase in the average life span. Aside from the fact that this shift leads to an undesired increase in the average age of the population, the death rate cannot go on falling forever, since we cannot abolish death and illness.

If the birthrate of the last decade were to continue—between 1900 and 1933, the annual number of births fell from two million to one million, which means it has fallen by half—a substantial decline in Germany's population would over time be inevitable. The German Office of Statistics estimates that the population of the German Reich would fall to about forty-seven million by the year 2000, and continue to fall thereafter, until another, stronger people would move into the empty space and our Germany would vanish from history like the old Greeks and other cultures of the past.

You know that since the takeover of power, there has been a happy improvement in the catastrophic population decline that had until then prevailed. The number of marriages, which had fallen to 517,000 in 1932, rose to 639,000 in 1933, 739,000 in 1934, and 651,000 in 1935.

The number of births per thousand reached its lowest point in 1933 at 14.7, or 971,000. In 1934 it rose for the first time in a long while to 1,197,000, or 18 per thousand, an increase of about a quarter. Despite a substantial decline in the number of marriages, the number of births rose again to 1,261,000, or 18.9 per thousand of the population. That is a very good situation that we can be more than proud of, since it shows unexpected and genuine confidence in the government leadership and in the political and economic future.

GERHARD WAGNER

Still, those voices both at home and abroad—I remember, for example, a recent article in Mussolini's paper *Popolo d'Italia*—are premature in drawing the conclusion that the German people has already resolved its population crisis. Aside from the fact that a birthrate of twenty per thousand is necessary to maintain our population, a figure that we have not yet reached, we have to expect a significant reduction in the number of marriages in coming years, which is the result of a not insignificant decline in the war and postwar generations that are now reaching marrying age. Thirty years of a declining birthrate have cost Germany around thirteen million unborn children. That cannot be undone. From the standpoint of racial hygiene, a particularly painful and serious loss is the 3 to 3.5 million children who would have been born to the best of our people, those who fell on the field of honor. They now would have been married and had children, the mothers and fathers of a strong generation.

The statistics of the first quarter of 1936 show that the declining marriage rate of 1935 is continuing. There were 10.4 percent fewer marriages than in the first quarter of 1935. At the same time, the statistics also prove the very happy fact that, just as last year, the decline of the birthrate has not been parallel to the decline in the marriage rate. It fell by only 1.4 percent, a bit less than last year.

All of our efforts and policies must aim at maintaining these favorable birth statistics, and strengthening them.

The critical question is whether we can succeed in reaching an average of three to four live births per marriage. Only that will guarantee the survival of our people. The duty of the state is to provide legal and especially economic measures to equalize the burdens that today fall particularly heavily on families with many children. The task of the movement will continue to teach the people through a powerful campaign of education and enlightenment that the path to the future leads through a generation of healthy children, a generation large enough to maintain—and if necessary—defend what their parents and ancestors have won and created. The deepest causes of the decline in the birthrate are not economic. They are spiritual; they are rooted in the hostile attitude of the past era to families and children. If we do not succeed in changing this internal attitude of the German people, all our population policy efforts—however generous they may be—will be useless and without hope.

Only when the German people joins its powerful political will for self-assertion to a determined affirmation of its will to life, to the maintenance of its population both in number and in kind, will it guarantee its military strength, its freedom, its honor, and its future for all time.

NOTES

1. For a good summary of the "positive" side of Nazi racial policy, see Claudia Koonz, *The Nazi Conscience* (Cambridge, Mass.: Harvard University Press, 2003).

2. The source is Gerhard Wagner, "Rasse und Bevölkerungspolitik," in *Der Parteitag der Ehre vom 8. bis 14. September 1936: Offizieller Bericht über den Verlauf des Reichsparteitages mit sämtlichen Kongreßreden* (Munich: Franz Eher, 1936), 150–61.

3. Duffee was a Catholic high school teacher who was not particularly well known, and the brief *New York Times* article discussing him appeared on 12 July 1936.

Joseph Goebbels

"Our Hitler": Speech on Hitler's 48th Birthday

19 APRIL 1937

Each year from 1933 to 1945, with the exception of 1934, Joseph Goebbels delivered a radio speech on the eve of Hitler's birthday, 20 April. The speech was carried in every major newspaper, and most were reprinted in collections of Goebbels's work. Each speech concluded with some variant of the phrase that ends this speech: "May he remain to us what he always was and is: Our Hitler!"

Goebbels's goal was to present Hitler as almost a Christ figure, divine (or at least superhuman), yet also human. This was part of the overall Nazi propaganda campaign about Hitler. He was not presented as an ordinary human, but rather as an historically unprecedented person with near miraculous strengths. More than a dozen books of photographs of Hitler were published in huge editions. "Heil Hitler" became the expected greeting in Germany. Thousands of poems were written in his honor. Many were hymns of praise. Yet he was also presented as a warm, loving human being, deeply concerned about each German.

Some of Goebbels's birthday speeches focused on the "superhuman" side of Hitler, others more on the personal, but each paid some attention to both aspects of the Hitler myth. The first speech in 1933 provided a "personal" portrait of Hitler, who had been in power only three months at the time. Later speeches worked to develop the myth of an all-knowing, all-wise leader. The final speech, delivered as Russian troops were nearing Berlin, promised that Hitler would, somehow, still win the war.

By 1937, Hitler had been in power for four years. His major territorial triumphs were yet to come, but already he had remilitarized the Rhineland, part of Germany that, under the Treaty of Versailles, was to remain free of German troops. The Saar district had voted overwhelmingly to return to full German control. The German economy was considerably stronger than it had been in 1933, and unemployment had almost vanished.

In this speech, Goebbels emphasizes the "divine" nature of Hitler. He is called a "genius" who knows more than the experts in every area of human knowledge, a person of penetrating wisdom, a leader of historic stature. Yet Goebbels also says that Hitler is deeply loved by the whole German people because of his humanity, because of his suffering for the nation. Part of Goebbels's goal was to create the impression that Hitler was universally popular, thus making those less certain of his virtues reluctant to risk saying anything in public.

Although it is difficult today to understand how Goebbels's inflated praise of Hitler could be taken seriously, it was. One way to understand Hitler's appeal to Germans, perhaps, is to imagine that one is hearing the speech in a context in which everything Goebbels says seems reasonable, and everyone around seems to agree.

SPEECH DELIVERED ON HITLER'S BIRTHDAY

My fellow people's comrades!

There are words the Führer has spoken that are unforgettable for the German people.[1] They live beyond the moment and its particular significance. Among these are the words he spoke on 8 November 1936 to his old fighting comrades in the Munich Bürgerbräukeller.[2] He described the great difficulties that he faced in fighting for the renewal of German freedom and security. To breathless silence, he then said that for the first time in his political life, his work had progressed to the point that he could look to the future without grave concerns. That was deeply moving not only for us, his old fighting comrades and companions, but for the entire German people. We shared one of those rare moments in which the Führer opens his heart to the nation and reveals his private thoughts. Each German suddenly had a personal insight into the great historic mission that the Führer had fulfilled, depending entirely and only on himself.

People in the democracies sometimes say that authoritarian governments have it easy. They do not need to worry about parties and parliaments, but rather make the decisions they think best and are not hindered by any majority or minority. In truth, that is hard, not easy. An authoritarian leadership certainly enjoys freedom of action. If it takes its responsibilities seriously, however, it has more to bear than the governments of parliamentary democracies. It has not only the power, but also sole and full responsibility. If problems mount up and there seems no escape from the difficulties, it cannot resign. It cannot hide behind an anonymous parliamentary majority that has no true responsibility. It stands or falls according to its historic mission; like the soldier in war, it must stand at its post.

Such responsibility is too heavy for an individual to bear, were not the people behind him. That is why the Führer saw his first political task as seeking out the entirety of the people and going with them on his tiring and thorny path. Perhaps it was good that the people did not immediately fall into his arms, that he had to fight bitterly for fourteen years to win the nation. Only thus did the nation come to belong to him so thoroughly and completely today.

There are men whom the people fear, men whom they respect, men whom they honor. But the greatest fortune of an historic personality is to be loved by a people. The greatest honor a man can hold is to be so bound and united with his people that he can at any time and in any situation speak in its name.

That is the case with the Führer. He is in fact the bearer of the German national will. His voice is the voice of the people.

People often ask for an explanation of this wonderful miracle. Evil-minded critics abroad would like the world to believe that it is a matter of conscious and determined popularity chasing. They know neither the Führer nor the German people. During Germany's democratic episode from 1918 to 1933, popularity was in fact chased. The parliamentary governments found no means too tasteless or too crude. But the nation failed to support them, viewing them only with contempt, scorn, and mockery. The Führer, to the contrary, has simply and steadily done his duty since he has stood at the head of the people, placing the full force of his strong heart in service of his historic mission. He has worked for his great goals without posturing or big talking. He has acted where others only talked. He spoke where others were silent. In his own cause he not only spoke, but rather let his actions speak for him. His actions are not determined by the nervous haste of the nine-day wonder who reaches for momentary success because he has missed the decisive opportunity. Never before has Germany taken such a long view as today. And never before has there been a man who worked at the head of the nation in so calm and disciplined a manner and in so sensitive and clear a way.

In all that happens in Germany today, whether economically, socially, or culturally, whether domestically or in foreign policy, one senses clearly that behind it all is the ordering and ruling hand of the Führer. There is no area of public life that is hidden from him, or with which he is unfamiliar. His clear gaze reaches far, and he is involved in everything that happens.

He is the best expert one can imagine. It is entirely impossible to deceive him with Potemkin villages.

There are those who have learned that by guiding him through exhibitions, or by giving speeches at conferences about future plans and projects. Perhaps they believed they were on safe ground, but they soon learned to their shame and embarrassment that even the tiniest error in statistics or facts was immediately noted. Suddenly they found themselves in an unexpected cross-fire of questions that displayed a startling understanding and surprising knowledge of an apparently esoteric topic.

A genius is able to see what is essential in things, situations, and people, to leave the nonessential to the experts, to think in fundamentals, and to carry the fundamentals through amidst a confusing mass of specialized knowledge. The Führer has this ability in great measure. His greatest gift is to distinguish the essential from the nonessential. He has an astonishing memory that always amazes even his closest comrades. He knows the important dates of Greek, Roman, English, French, and of course Prussian and German history. He knows even the most obscure names in every area of human activity. Without a moment's thought, he can draw the outlines of the Paris Opera, the Viennese Parliament, or Dresden's Zwinger Opera.

During many discussions on the rebuilding of the Reich capital, we saw that he knows Berlin better than any Berliner.

He understands every modern weapon. He knows the tonnage of all warships, our own, of course, but also those of foreign nations.

He is, one might say, a specialist in every area, but the wonderful thing is that while most specialists never go beyond their knowledge, his knowledge is the raw material for understanding and action.

His victories have stature.

Recently in a speech to a small group of his *Gauleiter*,[3] he quoted Field Marshall von Schlieffen's distinction between ordinary and great victories. His victories are of the latter variety. He does not like feuds to break out, and hates bombastic phrases that can only benefit our many enemies. He seeks his enemies out and joins battle when it is unavoidable; then he brings to bear his full strength and energy. He does not concern himself with minor, ordinary problems. He chooses tasks that are worth his while, and solves them in ways that are always simple and surprising. The victories he wins are truly grand. That is true above all of his successes in foreign policy, which even his most stubborn critics abroad cannot deny him.

Flexible tactics—firm principles.

Typical of his working style is to go to the heart of a matter, ignoring trivial and side issues. Tactics are always only the means to an end. But his political strategy is aimed at great national goals. It rests on firm moral foundations that are realized step by step, proving that great politics does not ruin character, but rather makes it hard and firm.

Fools are mostly stubborn both in tactics and principles. Intelligent and experienced political strategy, to the contrary, follows a clear and direct set of principles, but uses flexible tactics that change according to the situation. They are elastic and adjustable.

During the past four years, we have an unbroken and effective example of this in the Führer's work. During the first stages, he certainly had to make some risky decisions. Nothing would be more unjust, however, than to think he made such a decision carelessly, even once. Before every action, in worried days and sleepless nights, he thought through every option and possibility. Once he made a decision to act, he acted as a man confident in his guiding star.

Only his closest comrades know of the unending worries, worries that at times seemed unbearable. Only they know of the nervous and tortured hours when he alone bore the full responsibility.

The successes in all areas of our political life that seem almost self-evident to us today are the fruit of what came before. A united people, a strong nation in possession of weapons and able to defend its territory and honor, these are towering monuments. Every day, and on holidays, the people surround him with all their love. This perhaps springs from a need to be near to him, to live with him, to share his worries. This love comes to clearest expression during exciting national holidays or in trying times, times when he belongs to the whole nation.

Today is such a holiday. The whole nation joins in celebrating his 48th birthday. A flood of love, confidence, devotion, and thankfulness flows toward him. The mountains of letters and telegrams, the countless gifts that even today, and more so tomorrow, will pour into the Reich Chancellery in Berlin give evidence of this love. They all carry the same wish, whether spoken or unspoken. One might almost say it is the prayer of the nation to the Almighty: May the Führer remain with us in strength, health, and power for many years as the flag bearer of the people, as the first among the millions of workers, soldiers, farmers, and citizens, as the friend and protector of the youth, the patron of the arts, the supporter of culture and science, the architect of the united new nation!

We, his closest comrades, stand beside him on his day of honor. We lay our whole love and strong confidence at his feet. We are of one heart and one mind with him and the whole nation. We are filled with wonderful joy to know that one of the great ones of our

JOSEPH GOEBBELS

history is with us, to know that we serve and help him in his work that will survive the ages.

Under his hand, Germany has lifted itself from shame and impotence. The German people, encouraged and called by him, are once more aware of their mission. We all share the happy feeling of working to realize an ideal that makes life worth living.

The Germany that bears his name will be great and strong. Its people will again learn to be a great people and to act accordingly. Our children and children's children will find in it the homeland that encompasses all the Germans of the world, the strong protector of our life, our nature, and our work.

From all the Reich, from all German hearts on every continent, in foreign nations and on the wide oceans, the thanks and praise of millions rise united. May he remain to us what he always was and is: Our Hitler!

NOTES

1. The source is Joseph Goebbels, *Wetterleuchten. Aufsätze aus der Kampfzeit* (Munich: Franz Eher, 1939), 388–92. Goebbels's other birthday speeches are available on the GPA.
2. The site of Hitler's failed 1923 Beer Hall Putsch.
3. Nazi regional leaders.

Julius Streicher

Speech after "The Night of Broken Glass"

Julius Streicher (1885–1946) was among Hitler's earliest followers, and the most prominent and crudest Nazi anti-Semite.
He published the weekly newspaper *Der Stürmer* between 1923
and 1945, each issue of which was devoted entirely to revolting
anti-Semitic propaganda.[1] Streicher was also *Gauleiter*, or regional leader, of the Nazi Party in Nuremberg. He was executed for
crimes against humanity by the Nuremberg International Military Tribunal after World War II.

On 7 November 1938, Ernst vom Rath, a German diplomat in
Paris, was shot in Paris by a seventeen-year-old Jew whose family
had been the victim of Nazi anti-Semitic policies. Vom Rath died
of his wounds on 9 November. The Nazis, led by Joseph Goebbels and with Hitler's approval, organized nationwide attacks on
Jews in Germany, later called *Kristallnacht*, or the "Night of Broken Glass." Throughout Germany, over 1,500 synagogues were
burned down, thousands of Jewish shops were destroyed, dozens
of Jews were killed, and tens of thousands arrested. The Nazis
presented the violence as the "spontaneous" reaction of the German populace to vom Rath's murder. The main Jewish synagogue
in Nuremberg had been torn down three months before, but organized mobs destroyed another synagogue and ruined many
Jewish homes and offices. At least a dozen Nuremberg Jews were
killed or committed suicide.

Julius Streicher delivered this speech to a crowd of almost
100,000 on the day after the violence at "Adolf Hitler Square,"

a large public space in the center of Nuremberg. Although not a speech that had significant preparation, Streicher clearly summarized the anti-Semitic views that he had been proclaiming for twenty years. He claimed that all Jews were part of an international conspiracy to dominate the world. Since Germany was the leading anti-Semitic force in the world, the Jews hated Germany, and were attempting to organize a world coalition to destroy it. Rather than deploring the violence, Streicher praised the audience for its discipline, and criticized those who showed any sympathy for the Jews. Their violence, he asserted, was justified self-defense. He even promised that the audience would benefit from the redistribution of Jewish property. However, he also instructed the audience that there should be no further violence. Hitler would decide what had to be done next.

The newspaper account of the speech claimed that it was greeted with "a hurricane of enthusiasm." The aftermath of Kristallnacht, however, ended Streicher's political career. He had earlier offended Hermann Göring, who organized an investigation into what had happened to confiscated Jewish property in Nuremberg. Despite Streicher's claim in this speech that much of it would go to impoverished German families, the investigative committee found enormous financial irregularities, which finally persuaded Hitler to relieve Streicher of his position as *Gauleiter*, although Hitler permitted him to publish *Der Stürmer* until the end of the war (the last issue appeared in February 1945).

SPEECH DELIVERED THE DAY AFTER "THE NIGHT OF BROKEN GLASS"

Fellow people's comrades!

To begin, let us make this clear: You were not ordered to come here, but came of your own free will.[2] It is a shame that it is impossible for all those curious people abroad, and all those within our county who are the secret friends of certain forces abroad, cannot stand where I am standing to see for themselves how great the will of the people of Nuremberg and Franconia is to know the truth. You want to and shall hear the truth, and from those who have preached it for twenty years, not only in Franconia, but also to the entire world.

What happened? As the Führer last Monday paused here in Nuremberg while traveling to Munich, the news came from Paris that a seventeen-year-old Jew went into the German embassy and shot Counsel vom Rath. The whole world quickly heard the news. Those who do not understand the racial question, which is the key to everything, said what all ignorant people say: Someone mentally ill, a stupid young boy who did not know what he was doing, shot someone. For those of us with understanding, however, the shots in the Paris embassy meant something different than they did to those who never want to see. We know: That Jew was the representative and agent of the Jewish people, both through blood and education.

Parisian newspapers with the courage to print the truth have said that at his first interrogation, he answered the question of why he had done the deed by saying that an irresistible drive had made him go to the German embassy and shoot a German. We know where the drive that made the Jew shoot the German comes from. We know that the Jew received his blood from all the races of the world. Negro blood, Mongolian blood, Nordic blood, Indian blood—the blood of all races flows in this bastard race. This mixed blood forces the Jew into criminal deeds. As the old German proverb has it: "He who has mixed blood in his veins follows the worst direction." That means that he is forced to do wrong. He who has pure blood has a single soul; he who has mixed blood has a divided soul. Sometimes he obeys the good blood, sometimes the bad. As a bastard, the Jew always follows the dictates of his bad blood.

Thus, this creature went to the German embassy and shot the German counsel in the service of the Jewish people because his inferior mixed blood demanded it of him. His divided soul needed the death of this man, and this insolent Jewish murderer declared that he was sorry that the counsel was not dead, only wounded. Those French newspapers with the courage to tell the truth report to us that this Jewish murderer stated during his interrogation that he had been a student at a rabbinical school in Frankfurt. For twenty years, I have told the citizens of Nuremberg and Franconia that he who has gone to a rabbinical school has been educated not to the good, but to criminality. From his earliest childhood, the Jew is taught different things than we are taught. No, he is not taught "Love your neighbor as yourself" or "If someone strikes you on your right cheek, turn also your left cheek to him." Instead, he is taught: "You may do whatever you wish to a Gentile." He is even taught to see the execution of a Gentile as a deed that pleases God. We have been writing that in the *Stürmer* for twenty years, we have been preaching it to the whole world for twenty years, and we have brought an understanding of the Jewish Question to millions.

Still, we know that there are individuals among us who still have pity for the Jews, individuals who are not worthy to live in this city, not worthy to belong to this people of which you are a proud part. Today we heard of a "lady" who sighed that it was heartbreaking to see all the destroyed shops. Who had pity for us when, after the war, the Jew brought down enormous misery on the German people, as the Jew stole our savings during the great inflation, as Germany was blockaded during the World War by Jewish orders and hundreds of thousands of women and children starved? We are used to speaking our mind, and I say that those who behave like that "lady" do not belong here among us, and they can go wherever they want to with the Jews. We do not need them here!

We have done what we once said and prophesied that we would do. As I said to you twenty years ago, the time will come when Germans no longer live in barracks, but rather the Jews. Germans will then move into the fine houses. And if the Jews now move away, we will be able to give pleasure to some families with many children by allowing them to celebrate Christmas in a decent home, a home in which others previously celebrated a different holiday. The mayor will see to it that everything possible is done in the near future to relieve our present housing shortage. And the Führer has assured us that, especially in Nuremberg, more will be done to alleviate the tragic inheritance others left to us. The good will is there, but you all know the state Germany was in, and what must be done to make us secure. The Führer knows that the German people will bear everything proudly, including the poverty that still exists, in order to preserve our people as a whole.

It was mixed blood and education that drove the young Jew to murder. The Jew is educated to hate all Gentiles. However, the Jew also makes distinctions. It is no accident that the boy went into the German embassy instead of the Soviet-Russian embassy, or the American, or some other one.

Why did he choose the German embassy? He wanted to strike someone belonging to the people that the Jews hate most fervently.

At the end of September, the Jews in Germany were overjoyed, they were ecstatic. The Jews in the whole world were so happy that they could hardly control themselves. They hoped that the new world war that they had been dreaming and writing about for years was finally coming. They believed that they would then be able to regain their strength in Germany, or to return to it.

We could have killed all the Jews in Germany yesterday, but we did not do it. The demonstrations in Franconia were, in general, disciplined, clear, and farsighted. They proved to the world that the days when the Jew could take out his wrath on us, whether from within or without, are finally over. They showed a world friendly to the Jews that, when necessary, the German people can do whatever has to be done. And National Socialism has proven that when it acts with determination, it is successful.

What happened between yesterday and today has become history. The people demonstrated, and today the government declared that it wants the demonstrations to end. At the same time, it was announced that the Jews, who provoked the German people through their agent in Paris, will be subjected to new measures. They could have spared themselves those measures, but which now are necessary.

The Jew who fired the shot in Paris is not the only one who intended to take aim at the German people. The Jew in Paris, in the name of Jewry, wanted to strike symbolically at the heart of the German people. A short time ago, a Jew here told the police that Nuremberg Jews might attack political figures. He wanted to say that, if such a thing should happen, all Jews should not be held responsible. We believe in powers, whether human or of fate, that make revolver bullets and knives powerless. The Führer and his fellow fighters escaped bullets in front of the Feldherrnhalle. And I believe that, were a Jew to attack a leading political figure in Nuremberg, nothing could stop the Franconian people from finally solving the Jewish Question in Nuremberg. I believe that if the Jews were to do what they would like to do—as did the Jew Hirsch some years ago with his hellish machine[3]—Nuremberg's workers would say: "An eye for an eye, a tooth for a tooth!"

Let no one believe, however, that we were worried about that. We are subject to fate, we have fought for twenty years, and we move into the future with cheerful courage. We go on as people who know. We always want to come together to learn.

Do not forget that this murderer is a Jew. The Jew has the murder of Golgotha on his conscience. This people cannot be a "chosen" people. Nuremberg's teachers have decided that, in the future, they will teach children only those words that come from Christ's mouth. They refuse to teach the children any longer about a holy people of God.

In one night, the Jew butchered 75,000 Persians.[4] As he left Egypt, he killed all the firstborn, that means the whole posterity, of Egypt. What would have happened if the Jew had succeeded inciting the peoples into a war against us, and if we had lost that war? Under the protection of foreign bayonets the Jew would have butchered and murdered us. Never forget what history teaches.

The Jews would have instituted a new Purim festival in Germany. In celebrations abroad, they already use a doll to represent Adolf Hitler. With howls of glee from Jews old and young, it is taken to the gallows. But the hopes of the Jews have not been fulfilled, since we are not cowards, because we are National Socialists, because we no longer have parties or classes, because workers, factory workers, help to create this greater Germany, and because it has our full admiration. It also has my love and my admiration! I could not have survived these twenty years had you not supported me, had you not been so decent from the beginning. How many of you heard me in the Hercules Hall and today have changed inwardly because you believed what I said back then: "Look at those who want to be your leaders. They are Jews!"

The Nuremberg worker is farsighted, and no coward. He goes along proudly, quietly, and strongly! The Führer has often said: "If I had not had my workers, my craftsmen, I could not have carried out my work." He knew that he could rely on you.

What was the meaning of that bullet in Paris? Symbolically, it was aimed at the new National Socialist Germany's heart. The Jew wanted to say: "When the time comes, this whole people will be hit by a bullet. "They sent a seventeen-year-old Jew because they thought a French court would treat him gently. They hoped he would get a judge like the Jew Schwarzbart found ten or fifteen years ago.[5] He gunned down a Ukrainian leader, and was acquitted because the Ukrainian was a leader of a people that hated Jews. We do not know what the court will rule in this case. The new Germany waits for the verdict, the new Germany that is led by Adolf Hitler and owes its life to National Socialism.

The synagogue of Nuremberg's Jews once stood where we now stand. Nuremberg citizens set the synagogue on fire [in 1347], for it was not a house of God, but rather a den of murderers. We admire those men today, and say that they lived in a great era. In centuries to come, people will say that our age is a great age, too. The name of the man who fell to the murderous bullet will also go down in history. His name will join the names of those that are holy to us. Sixteen fell at the Feldherrnhalle.[6] Their blood sanctifies our flags. That is how we should see the death of Counsel vom Rath.

Our hope is that the Jewish people will one day receive the penalty they deserve for all the sorrow, misery, and trouble they have brought the peoples. We believe the supreme court is coming that will judge the Devil's people. Then the world will breathe more easily, and there will be peace.

And now I ask you to keep disciplined. No more demonstrations! We have made some progress, and will leave the rest to the Führer. We greet him with our Sieg Heil!

NOTES

1. See Randall Bytwerk, *Julius Streicher*, 2d ed. (New York: Cooper Square Press, 2001).
2. The source is "Einmal wird das Hochgericht kommen für das jüdische Volk," *Fränkische Tageszeitung*, 11 November 1938, 2–3.
3. Streicher's newspaper *Der Stürmer* had accused Hirsch, a Jew, of sexual crimes and perjury.
4. The story is in the biblical book of Esther, chapters 8–9.
5. Schlomo Schwartzbart, a Ukrainian Jewish anarchist, shot Symon Petlyura in Paris in 1926. Petlyura had ruled the Ukraine during a period of anti-Semitic pogroms that had killed fifteen members of Schwartzbart's family. A Paris jury accepted his defense that in killing Petlyura, he was avenging those deaths.
6. The site in Munich where Hitler's Beer Hall Putsch collapsed under police gunfire in 1923.

Adolf Hitler

Speech to the Old Guard in Munich

8 NOVEMBER 1941

Hitler spoke annually at three key dates on the Nazi calendar: 30 January, the anniversary of his takeover of power in 1933, 24 February, the anniversary of the proclamation of the party platform in 1920, and on the evening of 8 November to commemorate his 1923 attempt to take power by a revolution (the "Beer Hall Putsch"). The immediate audience for the 8 November speech consisted of his oldest followers, and was held in the same hall from which he had begun his abortive revolt, but the speech was also broadcast over the radio and printed in every daily newspaper.

In November 1941, Hitler was at the height of his success. In 1940, he had conquered Europe. In June 1941, he had invaded the Soviet Union, and his armies had made enormous territorial gains. The United States was still not in the war. The *Völkischer Beobachter*, the Nazi Party's daily newspaper, carried an article in October 1941 that announced victory.[1] Hitler reinforces the claim by asserting in this speech that Russia could never recover from the losses it had suffered. "Never before," he says, "has a vast empire been destroyed and defeated in so short a time as Russia has been." The regular Nazi slogan was "The Führer is always right," and most Germans believed that the end of the war was in sight, for how could England continue to stand alone once Russia was defeated?

In his usual style, Hitler provides an historical overview of his past actions, claiming that his actions in the past had always been correct. He takes the audience into his confidence, revealing his allegedly private thinking when he was making his decisions. The speech further provides examples of Hitler's style of humor (e.g., "The speed of our advance is determined not by those wonderful British strategists who have determined the speed of their retreats, but rather by we ourselves!").

Hitler also discussed the Jews. Between the beginning of the war and the invasion of the Soviet Union, he had been relatively silent about the Jews. The main enemy had been England, even if Nazi propaganda argued that the Jews controlled England from behind the scenes. After June 1941, however, the full force of Nazi propaganda turned toward the Jews, accusing them of planning to destroy Germany. In this speech, Hitler claims that he had acted only at the last possible moment to prevent such a fate. The Jews, he asserts, are "the arsonists of the world." They control the Soviet Union from behind the scenes.

As Hitler spoke, the Holocaust was in progress, and large numbers of Jews were being slaughtered in the east. Although the Nazis claimed they were out to destroy the Jews, they always kept the language general rather than specific. In this speech, Hitler asserts that "in areas we have occupied, we are polite and decent to the civilian population, perhaps too decent at times, very agreeable."

To the Old Guard in Munich

Party members! German people's comrades!

I arrived here a few hours ago, true to the old custom, to speak to you, my first followers and fellow fighters, and to honor those who made the greatest sacrifice that they could make for our movement, and for Germany.[2] I stood here before you last year after a glorious year of great accomplishments. I do not know how many outside the Reich had a clear idea of what might, and what did, happen during the year 1940. Even within our own people, there were probably very few who understood what was ahead, what would have to happen, what would happen.

After my last attempts in 1939 to make the necessary changes for peace had collapsed, and after the international democratic agitators had finally succeeded in plunging Europe into war, our first task was to deal with the enemy in the East. That took eighteen days. Those whose understanding had not completely deserted them should have been able to see after these few weeks how hopeless their attempts to defeat the German Reich once more were. They did not, however. To the contrary, when I extended the olive branch it was rejected. I myself was insulted and called a coward. There was nothing left for the year 1940 but to begin a final reckoning with the western opponent of the Reich.

Only through the carelessness, the talkativeness, of our opponents did we learn that they planned an attack on Norway, under the pretext of assisting Finland. They were really after the Swedish railroad and iron mines. Even then, they had not planned on our, and my, decisiveness. They had formed a picture of my personality based on those émigrés who had to leave Germany because of my personality. This picture was not entirely accurate. In fact, it was wrong. Contrary to what opponents expected, I very quickly decided to solve the Norwegian question in our way. We succeeded. A short time later came that unparalleled campaign that defeated the opponent in the West and forced England to that "glorious" retreat that will forever be, they say, one of the glorious deeds in British military history. I personally saw the remains of this "glorious" action; they looked rather untidy.

I then decided for the last time—as I said then—to extend my hand once more to England, and said that a continuation of this war could make no sense for England, that there was nothing standing in the way of a reasonable peace, that there were no conflicts between Germany and England, save for those created only for artificial reasons. The crazy drunkard who has led England for the last several years saw in this only a new sign of my weakness. Once again, I was portrayed as a man pessimistic about the future, and who therefore did not want to continue the struggle. I did not see the future in a way other than it happened. However, I foresaw not only the glory, but also the sacrifice, and I wanted to spare all sides that sacrifice. Of course, I wanted to spare our own people most of all, but I also believed that, as victor, I could take the responsibility in my own hands. As I said, that was not understood by those who have never had to make a sacrifice themselves, and who also have no close contact with the sacrifices of their own people.

We therefore had no choice but to put on the helmet and follow the path that would free not only the German Reich, but all of Europe, from the dangers that threatened.

When I spoke to you the last time, my old party comrades, I could speak with a foretaste of a victory unlike any mortal before me. Yet I still had a major worry: I knew that behind all these world events, the ultimate cause is the arsonist who has always lived from conflicts between nations: the international Jew! I would no longer have been a National Socialist if I had forgotten this knowledge. We have followed this path for many years, and probably for the first time, we in the Reich have systematically and scientifically clarified this problem and phenomenon of humanity, rightly choosing the words of a leading Jew himself who said that the racial question is the key to world history.[3] We therefore knew exactly, and I knew above all, that the Jew was the driving force behind events, and that he—as always in history—found blockheads who were ready to aid him, or paid minions without character who wanted to do business, who were and are ready to spill blood for such business at any time.

I learned to see these Jews as the arsonists of the world. One could see how he used the press, radio, film, theater, and so forth, to slowly poison the peoples over the years, and one saw how his poison spread, how his financial interests advanced his cause. During the first days of the war, certain Englishmen—all stockholders in the armaments industry—openly said: "The war has to last at least three years. It will not end before three years!" That is what they said. It was understandable. They had invested their capital, and could not hope to amortize their investment in less than three years. That is almost incomprehensible for us National Socialists, my party comrades. But that is how it is in the democratic world. One is prime minister or war minister, and at the same time the owner of countless shares of stock in armaments factories. This clarifies the situation.

We once knew this opponent as the driving force behind our domestic conflicts. We faced this coalition: the black-red-gold mixture[4] of hypocrisy and the misuse of religion on the one hand, the interests of capital on another hand, and finally the real Jewish-Marxist interests. In hard battle, we completely defeated this coalition at home. Now we still faced the same enemy abroad, the instigator of the world coalition against the German people and against the German Reich. First it moved to Poland, then brought France, Belgium, Holland, and Norway under its control. From the beginning, England was a driving force. What was more understandable than that one day the force that was most clearly dominated by the Jewish spirit would attack us? Soviet Russia was Jewry's greatest servant. Time has proven what we National Socialists always said for many years: it is a state that slaughters its national intelligentsia, leaving only a soulless proletarian subhumanity subject to an enormous organization of Jewish commissars—that is slaveholders. There were often doubts—perhaps even in this state national tendencies could still suddenly triumph. One forgot that there was no one left to bear a conscious national perspective, that in the final analysis the man who is temporarily leader of the state is nothing but an instrument in the hands of all-powerful Jewry, that whether Stalin stands on stage or behind it, behind him are people like Kaganovitsch[5] and all those Jews who in their tens of thousands rule this powerful land.

As I spoke to you here last year, these grim developments were already unmistakably clear to me. While we were marching to the west, Soviet Russia was marching to our east. There came a time when our three divisions in East Prussia faced twenty-two Russian divisions in the Baltic states. And they increased from month to month. That was not concealed from us. Almost monthly, we could establish exactly where each individual unit was. There were also enormous construction efforts along our front, which also could not be missed. Over the course of a few months, not one hundred, but nine hundred airfields were planned, begun, and in part completed. One could figure out the purpose behind such a gigantic, staggering massing of the Russian air force. It was the foundation for a huge attack, the size of which one could determine from the vastness of the preparations. Parallel to this was an unprecedented increase in armaments production. New factories were built, factories that you, my fellow party members, can hardly imagine. Two years before there was only an agricultural village. Now, there was a factory with 65,000 workers. The workers lived in mud huts. There were otherwise only factories, and the administrative buildings of the GPU, which looked like palaces from the front, but in the rear consisted of cells for the most gruesome torments and tortures. Troops were moved to our borders not only from the interior of the country, but from the far east of this vast empire. The number of divisions reached 100, 120, 140, 150, 170, and more.

Given these alarming events, I invited Molotov to Berlin. You know the results of that meeting. There was no doubt any longer that Russia intended to act, this fall at the latest, possibly already in the summer. They demanded, I might say, that we open the door for their entry. Now, I am not one of those people who resemble certain animals that seek out their own butcher. I therefore sent Molotov on his way. I was now sure that the die had been cast, and that the worst had to be expected. This was confirmed above all by Russia's activity in the Balkans, by its underground activity that could not long be concealed, which we knew well enough from our own experience. Everywhere there were Bolshevist agents, everywhere new Jews, everywhere subversive literature. There was underground work that after a short while one could no longer conceal, and in the end did not even want to conceal. They also began new propaganda, aimed at us. It was not successful, given the effectiveness of National Socialism's efforts.

The moment finally came when the Russian attack had to be expected. Aside from a few divisions in Moscow, as a protection against its own people, and a few divisions in the Far East, there were no forces not on the Western front. And then there was the trouble in Serbia, encouraged by Russia. Bolshevist agitators and English emissaries led a Putsch, followed by a friendship treaty between Russia and Serbia. Stalin was convinced that this campaign might occupy us for a whole year, after which the time would come for him to attack us not only with weapons and materiel, but also with gigantic reserves of men. For the first time, I can now say that there was one other factor:

In 1939 and 1940, there were a large number of so-called secret sessions of the British House of Commons. In these secret sessions, the whiskey-besotted Mr. Churchill revealed his thoughts and hopes, and ultimately his conviction, namely that Russia was planning to march toward England, and that he had absolute proof from Mr. Cripps that it would be at most a year to a year and a half before Russia acted, that they had to hold out for at most another year to a year and a half. That was the reason for the otherwise inexplicable courage he displayed then. We had information, steady information, about that.

I drew the consequences from all of this. The first step was to free our southeastern flank. I can only say that, given what we know today, we can really thank Mussolini that he lanced this boil in 1940. We succeeded in the spring, really within a few weeks, in solving this problem with the help of the European states supporting us, finally clarifying the question. The campaign concluded with the glorious capture of Crete, and closing off the Dardanelles.

I have often spoken of our military's accomplishments. It has also performed gloriously in this campaign, and not only the army, but the Luftwaffe in particular.

Now I watched every movement of our great opponent in the East. During April and May, I might say, I was always at the observation post, watching everything that happened, determined to act at the moment when I saw the opponent move, and if necessary, to strike 24 hours ahead of him.

In the middle of June, the signs grew threatening, and by the last half of June there was no doubt that it was only a question of days, or perhaps weeks. I therefore gave the order for us to act immediately on 22 June. Believe me, my old party comrades, it was the hardest decision of my whole life, because I knew that it would bring us a hard battle, but I hoped that the chances of winning it were greater the sooner we acted before the other side.

What was the situation at that time? The west was secure. Let me say one thing immediately. There are brilliant politicians in our enemy's camp who now say that I knew that the West would not attack us, and thus I had the courage to attack the East. I can only say to these geniuses that they entirely fail to understand my intentions. I have always prepared things in the West so as to be ready for them at any time. If the gentlemen in England want to undertake an offensive in Norway, or on our German coast, or in Holland, or in Belgium, or in France, we say only: Go right ahead. You will leave more quickly than you came! These coasts are in a different state than they were a year ago. We have been at work, and with National Socialist thoroughness. The leader of a good part of this work—I need only say a single name—was our Todt.[6]

And the work continues steadily. You know me from the early days of our party. I have never stood still. Wherever ten batteries stood, we added five more to be sure, and if there were fifteen, we added five more, and so on. Our opponents themselves delivered enough guns.

We have left enough forces to be ready at any time. The enemy has not come. Fine. I do not want to shed blood. But if they had come—as I said—they would long since have left. Here, too, we were secure.

We also secured the Balkans. In North Africa, too, our common efforts succeeded in building a stable order. Finland declared itself ready to join our side. Rumania, too. Bulgaria saw the danger, and did nothing that would hinder us. Hungary also recognized the great historic moment and came to a heroic decision. When 22 June came, I believed we were ready to meet the danger—only a few days in advance.

This, my old party comrades, is a battle not only for Germany, but for all Europe, a battle of life or death!

You know our allies, beginning in the north with the brave little heroic Finnish people, who have proved themselves once again beyond all measure. But there are also the Slovaks, the Hungarians, the Rumanians, and also—you may not forget that this involves long marches, vast transport paths—allies from almost all of Europe: Italians, Croats, Dutch, Danish volunteers, Swedish volunteers, Norwegian volunteers, even French volunteers, Belgian volunteers. I can truthfully say that, perhaps for the first time in its history, all of Europe is fighting in the East. Once it fought against the Huns, this time against the Mongol state of a second Genghis Khan.

The goal of the battle was to destroy enemy power, that is, the enemy's military forces, and second, to occupy the enemy's armaments and agricultural regions. I need not tell you that questions of prestige played no role at all. If someone today says that we are on the defensive at Leningrad—well, we were on the offensive as long as it took to surround Leningrad. We are now on the defensive, but the other side will have to break out; he will starve in Leningrad, or he will capitulate! But I will sacrifice not one man more than is absolutely necessary.

If someone were to attempt to relieve Leningrad, I would give the order to storm it, and we would capture it. He who marched from East Prussia to ten kilometers outside Leningrad can also march the remaining ten kilometers. One can be sure of that.

That, however, is not necessary. The city is surrounded, no one can free it, and it will fall into our hands. If someone says: "Only in ruins," my reply is that I have no interest in a city named Leningrad, but rather only in the destruction of Leningrad's industry. If the Russians want to blow their cities up, they will perhaps save us the trouble. I repeat once again, party members, that prestige is not a concern. Or if someone asks: "Why do you not march now?"—Because it is raining at the moment, or snowing, or perhaps because we have not entirely finished the rail lines. The speed of our advance is determined not by those wonderful British strategists who determined the speed of their retreats, but rather by we ourselves!

Second, the occupation of enemy armaments and agricultural regions. Here, too, we proceed systematically! Sometimes, the destruction of a single factory is enough to cripple completely many others as well.

To summarize the results of this campaign so far, the number of captured has reached around 3.6 million, that is, 3.6 million prisoners. At least as many have been killed. And I will not permit some blockheaded Englishman to say that we do not have any proof of that. If a German military office has determined something, it is true! It is a different matter if some stock exchange swindler adds things up. There is a significant difference between a German officer and a British stockbroker. The numbers are accurate, just as were our figures about captured French soldiers.

They were exactly accurate. The English know that themselves, since they always were concerned about it.

If I consider 3.6 million prisoners in relation to the World War, I expect at least the same number of dead. It would be a bad sign for Mr. Stalin if his people today fought less bravely than they did during the World War. To the contrary, they fight partly from anxiety, partly from fear, and partly from a fanatic animalistic insanity. And if I assume that, just as with us, there are three to four wounded for every fatality, at the very least eight to ten million men have been wounded and are no longer available for combat, not including the lightly wounded who perhaps will recover completely.

My party members, no army in the world can recover from that, not even the Russian!

If Mr. Stalin suddenly says that we have lost 4 1/2 million, and Russia has only lost 350,000—350,000 dead and 1,000,000 wounded—then one asks: Why have the Russians retreated fifteen hundred kilometers, despite the fact that they have enormous numbers and only half the casualties that we have had?

In fact, the Kremlin is behaving in a strongly Jewish manner. By the way, these prisoners will gradually benefit European agriculture. We will use them in production, and one will then see that there are not 350,000 of them, but 3 1/2 million.

We have captured enormous amounts of military materiel. So far, over 15,000 aircraft, over 22,000 tanks, over 27,000 artillery pieces. There is a huge amount of it. The industry of the whole world, ours included, could only gradually replace it. The industries of our democracies, at least, will not replace it in the next few years!

And now I come to territory. We have so far occupied over 1,670,000 square kilometers. That is three or four times the size of France, about five times the size of England. This area includes 60 to 75 percent of all industries and raw materials that Russia possesses. I hope to make a few more steps in the near future, slowly but surely tightening the noose.

If someone now says: "Sure, but you misjudged the time"—people know exactly how I measure time! We defeated France in about six weeks. The occupied areas there are only a fraction of what we occupy in the East. Now someone comes and says we expected to march through the East in a month and a half. Now that would be a Blitzkrieg! But one still has to march.

And what our infantry has accomplished in the matter of marching is unprecedented in world history. I will grant that it is easier to march from Ostend to Dunkirk or from Dunkirk to Ostend. But when one marches from the German border to Rostov, or to the Crimea, or to Leningrad, those are real distances, particularly when one considers the roads in "the workers' and farmers' paradise." I have never used the word Blitzkrieg, since it is a foolish word. If one has to apply it to a campaign, however, then apply it to this one! Never before has a vast empire been destroyed and defeated in so short a time as Russia has been.

This could succeed only because of the unparalleled bravery and sacrifice, through the unimaginable exertions, of our German army. What German weapons have accomplished is in part unimaginable. We can only bow deeply before our heroes.

I previously said in Berlin that whether we consider our tank gunners, our engineers, our artillerymen, our intelligence troops, our pilots, our Stuka dive bombers, our reconnaissance planes, our fighter pilots—whomever we consider, in the end we must give the crown to the German infantryman, to the German musketeer. He marches along endless paths over soggy ground, through mire and swamps, through burning sun across the Ukraine's endless fields, and he captures bunker after bunker. With the help of his engineers, he plunges through front after front. It is really a heroic song that he sings.

Behind this front, however, stands a second front, the German home front. And behind the German home front stands a third front, and this is Europe. People have told me often recently that the democracies are arming. I have often said that we are not idle either, that I did not stop German armaments in 1939 or 1940 or 1941. What we accomplished in the past was everywhere clear. And we continue to arm, and thoroughly. And I have transferred German armaments production to certain areas. Other gentlemen may constantly proclaim numbers. I do not speak in numbers. I only say this: One day they will be astonished!

ADOLF HITLER

We experienced all this at home, too, my old party comrades. Each year we heard what the Democrats were doing, what the Social Democrats were doing, what the Center Party or the Bavarian People's Party were doing, what some bourgeois group or another was doing, and so forth, or even what the communists were doing. But we were doing something, too, more than all of them were together, and in the end we defeated the entire coalition!

Still, someone says to me: "But what about America, with its 125,000,000 people." The Reich, including the Protectorate and the Gouvernement,[7] also has 125,000,000 people! The area that is working directly for us includes far more than 250,000,000 people. And the parts of Europe working indirectly in this battle, our allies, already have over 350,000,000 people! Considering only German territory, the area that we have occupied, the area we now administer—no one should doubt that we will use it productively. One can be sure of that! This is no longer the Germany of the World War. It is an entirely different Germany. It is the misfortune of our opponents that they have not understood this, that they have believed the empty Jewish brains that constantly told them: "You just have to do what you did in the past." I do not do that, although I do not think my opponents very clever. Even I never do the same thing again, but always something different. They, too, should learn something new, and not always hope the old will work!

For example, they say: "There will be a revolt in the behind the lines." There may be some idiot who believes an English radio story. But not for long! We will deal with him. Revolts—one should not be deceived—will collapse very quickly, for today they do not face a bourgeois Germany that wears kid gloves, but rather one with tough National Socialist fists!

Wherever we are in areas we have occupied, we are polite and decent to the civilian populace, perhaps too decent at times, very agreeable. No one is raped by us, for many reasons. There are no thefts. The German soldier who steals or plunders will be punished more severely than he would be at home. We protect the civilian populace. If, however, someone believes he can resist our occupation, or perhaps shake it through cowardly murder, then we will respond as we responded at home in those years when our opponents believed that they could terrorize us. In the end, we were the master of terror, we created the organizations for it. And we will also deal with terror on the part of this opponent!

The most stupid hope is the idea that there will be an uprising, a revolution, in Germany. The people who could lead a revolution are no longer there. We do not have them any more. They are all in England and America and Canada, and so on. The people who would still like to cause one are so few and so harmless that it is almost a joke to depend on them. If any one of us still believes that he could disrupt our front, however, regardless of where he comes from or what camp he belongs to—you know my methods—I will watch him for a while. I give everyone a chance. He can be what he wants. I will watch for a time. But the moment will come when I act with lightning speed and deal with it quickly. No cover will help, not even the cover of religion. But as I said, that will not be necessary, since above all this whole German people is organized today in a movement that our opponent has not understood, a movement that reaches into every home and works to ensure that November 1918 does not repeat itself. I have often been a prophet during my life. I have often been laughed at, but have always proven right. Let me say once again: November 1918 will never repeat itself in Germany! It cannot repeat itself. Anything is possible except for this: that Germany will ever capitulate!

If our opponent says: "Well, then the war will last into 1942"—it can last as long as it wants—the last battalion on the field will be German! There is no point in trying to intimidate me. You know that I often am silent about something for months or years. That does not mean that I do not see it, that I do not notice it, that I do not recognize it. If there are new threats against Germany today, particularly from America, I keep it in mind. A year ago I said that if a ship is carrying war materiel, that is, materiel to kill people, it will be torpedoed! If American President Roosevelt, who was responsible for Poland's entry into the war, and who we can prove encouraged France to enter the war, believes that he can make us nervous by ordering his ships to shoot at ours, I give him this answer: President Roosevelt has ordered his ships to fire when they see Germans. I have ordered German ships not to fire on American ships that they see, but as soon as a German ship is attacked, it is to defend itself. I will court martial an officer who does not defend himself.

If, therefore, an American ship follows the president's orders and fires, it does so at its own risk. The German ship will defend itself, and our torpedoes hit their targets.

I do not concern myself with these ridiculous forgeries, for example, that we have fabricated a map, using experts, German experts. I can only say to Mr. Roosevelt: In certain areas, I do not have any experts. My own mind is enough. I do not need a brain trust to support me. If, therefore, something is to happen somewhere, it will come from my brain, not the brains of others. And I am not a schoolboy who plays with maps in an atlas. South America is the moon, as far as we are concerned. These are stupid, blatant forgeries.[8]

Then there is the charge that we want to eliminate all the world's religions. I am now fifty-two years old, and I have better things to do than to worry about childish matters or stupid things. I am not interested in the religions of the world, and who belongs to them. That is of interest only to American presidents like Wilson or Roosevelt, but not to me. In the German Reich, as we see it, each can choose whatever religion he wants.

I have read that it is illegal in America for a preacher to preach against the state, and for soldiers to attend such sermons. The same is true with us. By the way, there is one difference. In the German Reich, the various churches receive nearly 900,000,000 marks a year from the state, but not a penny in America! In the German Reich, a priest has never been prosecuted because of his beliefs, but only if he ignores his beliefs and interferes in matters of state. Only a very few have done that. The great majority, despite everything else, stands behind the German state. They know well that, at least under Stalin's protection, religion would fare worse than under us.

All other attempts to influence the German people from abroad are childish and ridiculous. The German people have known the National Socialist regime as a party for nearly twenty years, and as leader of the state for eight years. I do not believe there has ever been a time in German history when so much has been accomplished in eight years as has been accomplished in the

German Reich during eight years of National Socialist leadership.

The best witnesses of the effects of our movement, however, are those who return from the front and compare the results of twenty-three years of communism with our results. They can pass judgment on what National Socialism has accomplished, and what would happen to Europe if this other world should be victorious. And that is the great goal: that we finally eliminate the threat to Europe from the East, and that we no longer allow the immeasurable fruitfulness of the East, its enormous riches, its riches in minerals and ores, and so forth, to be mobilized against Europe, but rather that we put the East in the service of Europe.

That is a gigantic goal that reaches far beyond our party, beyond even our German Reich. It is gigantic not only in what it will take to achieve it, but also in the results. It is insane when we see that in Europe there are some regions—I need only to think of the west—in which as many as 260 people live on each square kilometer!

I see these things—I can probably say—from a higher point of view. I distinguish between the Frenchman and his Jews, between the Belgians and their Jews, between the Dutch and their Jews. I know that there are countless people who are also victims of this crazy European system, under which the richest part of Europe is constantly mobilized against that part of Europe where people have only the most primitive standard of living. Our soldiers have seen this: In a country with the most fruitful soil on earth, where only a fraction of the effort it takes here would produce far more, people have so little that they have but a single pot, live in miserable hovel. They are neglected, filthy, infected with lice. I read a few days ago that they found lice on a German prisoner of war. Mr. Stalin can say that if he wants. I assume that he will not believe that this prisoner brought these lice to Russia from Munich or Berlin. He got them there. It is really the most miserable slavery that one can imagine, frightened, oppressed, ruined people, half starved! Over them stands a regime of commissars, 90 percent of them Jews, who govern this slave state. It will be a blessing for Europe not only when this danger disappears, but when the richness of the earth and of the soil benefits all of Europe.

ADOLF HITLER

That is a great task we have before us, and I am enough of a materialist to consider it much more important than worrying about what religions prevail in America.

We have a goal that covers this continent, our fatherland primarily, but then to all those who face the same problems we do. And I am convinced that this continent will then not be the second in the world, but it will be, as in the past, the leading one. Herr Willke, that honest man, says that there are only two possibilities. Either Berlin will be the capital of the world, or Washington will be the capital of the world. I can only reply that Berlin does not want to be the capital of the world, and Washington will never be the capital of the world! I believe there would be fifty mid-sized cities in Europe that would protest against such a cultural insult to humanity.

This great goal, in the final analysis, is only the last step of our program that we once began, this reasonable program that depends on human labor, that puts people in the center of action, of striving, and that brings them fulfillment.

We then set the terms person, people's comrade, and labor over against the terms gold and capital, and today also we set the person and his labor against them. We include all those who today stand as our allies, above all the state that has suffered the same misery, indeed, in part even greater misery than Germany itself: Italy. The Duce—and I know this—sees this battle no differently than we do. His is a poor land, overpopulated, always disadvantaged, never knowing where its daily bread will come from. He and I have sworn an oath, and no power on earth can break that bond! There were two revolutions at different times, and in different forms, but with a common goal. They will reach their common goals together.

A large number of other European states have joined us. We can say that nearly the whole of southeastern Europe is in our camp, and that a great part of the rest of Europe is too, if not officially, at least in thinking.

We National Socialists today no longer fight alone, but rather in a strong European front. And at the end of this year, we can probably say that this European front has already defeated its greatest danger.

As I spoke recently in Berlin, we stood before the beginning of the last gigantic blow. It succeeded beyond all expectations. About seventy-five divisions were wiped out and destroyed in a single blow.

The leadership of this struggle, and its subordinates, will not weary or tire. The heroic courage of the front is immortal, and those of us who believe in Providence can also be sure that such an immortal deed will have an eternal reward.

We may have no doubt that Europe's future for the next thousand years is being decided. And we may all be happy that we live in these times, and that you, my friends from the old days, you may be proud that you found your way to me, who had been chosen by Providence to follow this path, that you followed a then unknown man as I began to follow my path in this city.

And in this year, we can stand at the graves of our comrades with even more pride than before. Last year, we might have been softly criticized. We all fought against the Red Front, but fate forced us to accept an armistice with the Red Front. I kept this armistice honestly. The other side freed us from this obligation. This year, I almost stand as one delivered before the graves of my party comrades, for I know that all these party comrades had the same goal: the battle against the world enemy, against the Marxist world enemy, and the battle against its allies. Back then, they fell to the bullets of a front that reached from stupid reactionaries to crazed, fanatic Bolshevists.

Especially in this year, we remember those who fell with deep respect and emotion. You will understand my feelings. I have been back in this city for only a few hours, the city from which I came, but I am so happy to see you again, my old comrades in arms, my old companions. And you may be sure that a great burden has been taken from my heart this year. I know the whole sacrifice that we have to bring: all of our many young and old friends who had to pay with their blood for Germany's salvation, or who perhaps will still have to pay.

It is the old, eternal struggle, the old, eternal battle. It found no end in 1918. Then we were robbed of victory. We sacrificed two million dead, we had over seven and a half million wounded, yet we were robbed of victory by the insanity of a revolution at home.

But that was only the beginning, the first act of this drama. The second and final acts are now being written, and we this time will gain what was stolen from us then. Point for point, position by position, the bill is being presented and paid. And this includes not only the sixteen men who fell before the Feldherrnhalle as the first blood martyrs of our movement, but also all the millions of others. They did not fall in vain.

The hour will come when we can also stand before their graves and say: "Comrades, you did not die in vain!" Once we said before the Feldherrnhalle: "You have won after all." With a thousand times more justice, we will stand before the graves of our soldiers of the World War and say: "Comrades, you have won after all!"

NOTES

1. "The Great Hour Has Come: The Campaign in the East Is Decided," *Völkischer Beobachter*, 10 October 1941, 1.

2. The source is *Der großdeutsche Freiheitskampf: III. Band, Reden Adolf Hitlers vom 16. März 1941 bis 15. März 1942* (Munich: Franz Eher, 1942), 89–109.

3. Hitler refers here to British Prime Minister Benjamin Disraeli.

4. The colors of leading political parties before Hitler took power.

5. Kaganovitsch was a leading Soviet Jewish political leader.

6. Fritz Todt was in charge of war production.

7. The German names for occupied Czechoslovakia and Poland.

8. The U.S. government had released what it claimed was a German map showing plans to take over South America. For more details, see an essay by Goebbels, http://www.calvin.edu/academic/cas/gpa/goeb2.htm.

Joseph Goebbels

"People, Rise Up, and Storm, Break Loose"

18 FEBRUARY 1943

Goebbels's "Total War" speech of 18 February 1943, may be the single most famous Nazi speech. It came at a turning point in the war. When Hitler spoke in November 1941, victory seemed sure. German armies were everywhere victorious. The winter of 1941–1942 was a shock. Hitler had not expected the Russians to hold out, and the German army was ill-prepared for winter. The Russians counterattacked. The German front shook—but held.

In summer 1942, the Germans gained additional ground, capturing most of the key city of Stalingrad, important both for its location and its name. But the Russians struck back in October 1942, surrounding the Germans in the ruined city. For several months, the German media said almost nothing about Stalingrad, until on 2 February 1943 the remaining German troops surrendered. For the first time, an average German could see that the war might be lost.

Goebbels for months had been trying to increase his control over the war effort, and the defeat at Stalingrad was his opportunity. He prepared a vivid speech to rouse German resistance and persuade Hitler to give him more power.

He chose the Berlin Sport Palace, the site of many previous Nazi rallies. It held about fourteen thousand people. Goebbels selected them carefully, securing the most fanatic audience he could find. It was a media event. The speech was broadcast in full twice on national radio, printed in all leading newspapers, reprinted in a mass pamphlet with a circulation in the millions, and five minutes of the speech, including its conclusion, were included in the newsreel of 24 February 1943, which was shown before the feature in every movie theater. No one in the Third Reich escaped this speech.

Both in the Sport Palace and in newsreel coverage, the impression was of a fanatic audience willing to do whatever necessary for victory. Goebbels declared that his audience was representative of the nation, a parliament of the people, and as he described the audience, the camera panned over soldiers, government officials, artists, civil servants, and women, all wildly enthusiastic.

Albert Speer, Hitler's architect and minister for war production, talked with Goebbels after the speech, and learned how carefully calculated the speech had been:

> Goebbels astonished me by analyzing what had seemed to be a purely emotional outburst in terms of its psychological effect—much as an experienced actor might have done. He was also satisfied with his audience that evening. "Did you notice? They reacted to the smallest nuance and applauded at just the right moments. It was the politically best-trained audience you can find in Germany."

Goebbels cynically went on to say that, had he told the audience to go to the top of a high building and jump off, they would have obeyed.[1]

Popular reaction to the speech was favorable, though some did see the methods Goebbels used. Hitler, too, was impressed, and Goebbels's standing rose.

Unlike other speeches in this collection, this text is based on the speech as delivered. Although copies were distributed to the press in advance, Goebbels made several points more strongly in his oral presentation than in the printed version. The most significant sections omitted from the printed text are in brackets.

My German people's comrades. Fellow party members.[2]

Only three weeks ago I stood in this place to read the Führer's proclamation on the tenth anniversary of the seizure of power, and to speak to you and to the German people. The crisis we now face on the Eastern Front was at its height. In the midst of the hard misfortunes the nation faced in the battle on the Volga, we gathered this year in a mass meeting on the 30th of January to display our unity, our unanimity, and our strong will to overcome the difficulties we faced in the fourth year of this war.

It was a moving experience for me, and probably also for all of you, to learn several days later that the last heroic fighters in Stalingrad had joined by radio our powerful meeting here in the Sport Palace. They radioed to us that they had heard the Führer's proclamation, and perhaps for the last time in their lives, joined us in raising their hands to sing the national anthems. What an example German soldiers have set in this great age! And what an obligation it puts on us all, particularly the entire German home-land! Stalingrad was and is fate's great alarm call to the German nation! A people that has the strength to survive and overcome such a misfortune, even to draw from it additional strength, is unbeatable. In my speech to you and the German people, I shall remember the heroes of Stalingrad, who put me, and all of us, under a deep obligation.

I do not know how many millions of people, at home and at the front, are participating in this mass meeting by listening to me over the radio tonight. I want to speak to all of you from the depths of my heart to the depths of yours. I believe that the entire German people has a passionate interest in what I have to say tonight. I will therefore speak with holy seriousness and openness, as the hour demands. The German people, raised, educated, and disciplined by National Socialism, can bear the whole truth. It knows the gravity of the situation the Reich is in, and its leadership can therefore demand the necessary hard measures, yes, even the hardest measures. We Germans are armed against weakness and uncertainty. The blows and misfortunes of the war only give us additional strength, firm resolve, and a spiritual and fighting will to overcome all difficulties and obstacles with revolutionary élan.

Now is not the time to ask how it all happened. That can wait until later, when the German people and the whole world will learn the full truth about the misfortune of the recent weeks, and its deep and fateful significance. The heroic sacrifice of our soldiers in Stalingrad has had vast historic significance for the whole Eastern Front. It was not in vain. The future will make clear why.

If I jump over the most recent past to look ahead, I do so intentionally. Time is short! There is no time for fruitless debates. We must act immediately, decisively, and thoroughly as has always been the National Socialist way.

The movement has from its beginning acted in that way to master the many crises it faced and overcame. The National Socialist state also acted decisively when faced by a threat. We are not like the ostrich that sticks its head in the sand so as not to see danger. We are brave enough to look danger in the face, to coolly and ruthlessly take its measure, then act decisively with our heads held high. Both as a movement and as a nation, we have always been at our best when we needed fanatic, determined wills to overcome and eliminate danger, or a strength of character sufficient to overcome every obstacle, or bitter determination to reach our goal, or a strong heart capable of withstanding every internal and external battle. So it will be today. My task is to give you an unvarnished picture of the situation, and to draw the hard conclusions that will guide the actions of the German government, but also of the German people.

We currently face a serious military challenge in the East. The challenge is at the moment a broad one, similar but not identical in many ways to that of last winter. Later we will discuss the causes. Now, we must accept things as they are and discover and apply ways and means to deal with the situation. There is no point in disputing the seriousness of the situation. I refuse to give you a false impression of the situation that could lead to false conclusions, perhaps giving the German people a false sense of security that is altogether inappropriate in the present situation.

The storm raging against our venerable continent from the steppes this winter overshadows all previous human and historical experience. The German army and its allies are the only possible defense. In his proclamation on 30 January, the Führer asked in a grave and compelling way what would have become of Germany and Europe if, on 30 January 1933, a bourgeois or democratic government had taken power instead of the National Socialist movement. What dangers would have followed, faster than even we could then have suspected, and what powers of defense would we have had to meet them? Ten years of National Socialism have been enough to make plain to the German people the seriousness of the danger posed by Bolshevism from the East. Now one can understand why we spoke so often of the fight against Bolshevism at our Nuremberg party rallies. We raised our voices in warning to our German people and the world, hoping to awaken Western humanity from the paralysis of will and spirit into which it had fallen. We tried to open their eyes to the horrible danger from Eastern Bolshevism, which had subjected a nation of nearly 200,000,000 people to the terror of the Jews and was preparing an aggressive war against Europe.

When the Führer ordered the German army to attack the East on 22 June 1941, we National Socialists knew that this would be the decisive battle of this great struggle. We knew the dangers and difficulties. But we also knew that dangers and difficulties always grow over time, they never diminish. It was two minutes before midnight! Waiting any longer could easily have led to the destruction of the Reich and a total Bolshevization of the European continent.

It is understandable that, as a result of wide-ranging deceptions and bluffs by the Bolshevist government, we did not properly evaluate the Soviet Union's war potential. Only now do we see its true scale. That is why the battle our soldiers face in the East exceeds in its hardness, dangers, and difficulties all human imagining. It demands our full national strength. This is a threat to the Reich and to the European continent that casts all previous dangers into the shadows. If we fail in this battle, we will have failed our historic mission. Everything we have built and done in the past pales in the face of this gigantic task that the German army directly, and the German people less directly, face.

I speak first to the world, and proclaim three theses regarding our battle against the Bolshevist danger in the East.

The first thesis: Were the German army not in a position to break the danger from the East, the Reich would fall to Bolshevism, and all Europe shortly afterwards.

The second thesis: The German army, the German people, and their allies alone have the strength to save Europe from this threat.

The third thesis: Danger faces us. We must act quickly and decisively, or it will be too late.

I turn to the first thesis. Bolshevism has always proclaimed its goal openly: to bring revolution not only to Europe, but also to the entire world, and plunge it into Bolshevist chaos. This goal has been evident from the beginning of the Bolshevist Soviet Union, and has been the ideological and practical goal of the Kremlin's policies. Clearly, the nearer Stalin and the other Soviet leaders believe they are to realizing their world-destroying objectives, the more they attempt to hide and conceal them.

We National Socialists cannot be fooled. We are not like those timid souls who wait like the hypnotized rabbit until the serpent devours them. We prefer to recognize the danger in good time and take effective action. We see through not only the ideology of Bolshevism, but also its practice, for we had great success with that in our domestic struggles. The Kremlin cannot deceive us. We had fourteen years of our struggle for power, and ten years thereafter, to unmask its intentions and its infamous deceptions. The goal of Bolshevism is Jewish world revolution. They want to bring chaos to the Reich and Europe, using the resulting hopelessness and desperation to establish their international, Bolshevist-concealed capitalist tyranny.

I do not need to say what that would mean for the German people. A Bolshevization of the Reich would mean the liquidation of our entire intelligentsia and leadership, and the descent of our workers into Bolshevist-Jewish slavery. That is their goal! In Moscow, they find the workers for forced labor battalions in the Siberian tundra, as the Führer said in his proclamation on 30 January. The revolt of the steppes is readying itself at the front, and the storm from the East that breaks against our lines daily in increasing strength is nothing other than a repetition of the historical devastation that has so often in the past endangered the life of our continent.

That is a direct threat [not only to our existence, but also] to every European power. No one should believe that Bolshevism would stop at the borders of the Reich, were it to be victorious, because of a treaty on paper. The goal of its aggressive policies and wars is the Bolshevization of every land and people in the world. In the face of such undeniable intentions, we are not impressed by paper declarations from the Kremlin or guarantees from London or Washington. We know that we are dealing in the East with an infernal political devilishness that does not recognize the norms governing relations between peoples and nations.

When, for example, the English Lord Beaverbrook says that Europe must be given over to the Soviets, or when the leading American Jewish journalist Brown cynically adds that a Bolshevization of Europe might solve all of the continent's problems, we know exactly what the Jews have in mind. The European powers are facing the most critical question of life itself. The West is in danger! It makes no difference whether or not their governments and intellectuals realize it is.

The German people, in any event, are unwilling to bow to this danger. Behind the oncoming Soviet divisions we see the Jewish liquidation commandos, and behind them terror, the specter of mass starvation, and complete anarchy in Europe. International Jewry is the devilish ferment of decomposition that finds cynical satisfaction in plunging the world into the deepest chaos and destroying ancient cultures that it played no role in building.

We also know our historic responsibility. Two thousand years of Western history are in danger. One cannot overestimate the danger. It is indicative that when one names it as it is, International Jewry throughout the world protests loudly. Things have gone so far in Europe that one cannot call a danger a danger when it is caused by the Jews! That does not stop us National Socialists from drawing the necessary conclusions. [We have never been afraid of the Jews, and are even less afraid today!]

That is what we did in our earlier domestic battles. The democratic Jewry of the *Berliner Tageblatt* and the *Vossische Zeitung* served communist Jewry by minimizing and downplaying a growing danger, and by lulling our threatened people to sleep and sapping its ability to resist. We foresee, if the danger is not overcome, the specter of hunger, misery, and forced labor by millions of Germans. We see our venerable part of the world collapsing, burying in its ruins the ancient inheritance of the West. That is the danger we face today.

My second thesis: Only the German Reich and its allies are in the position to resist this danger. The European nations, including England, believe that they are strong enough to resist effectively the Bolshevization of Europe, should it come to that. This belief is childish and not even worth refuting. If the strongest military force in the world, the German Reich, is not able to break the threat of Bolshevism, who else could do it? The neutral European nations have neither the potential nor the military means nor the spiritual strength to provide even the least resistance to Bolshevism. Bolshevism's robotic divisions would roll over them within a few days. In the capitals of the mid-sized and smaller European states, they console themselves with the idea that one must be intellectually armed against Bolshevism. That reminds us of the statements by bourgeois parties in 1932, who thought they could fight and win the battle against communism with intellectual weapons. That was too stupid even then to be worth refuting.

Eastern Bolshevism is not only a doctrine of terrorism, it is also the practice of terrorism. It strives for its goals with an infernal thoroughness, using every resource at its disposal, regardless of the welfare, prosperity, or peace of the peoples it ruthlessly oppresses. What would England and America do if, in the worst case, Europe fell into Bolshevism's arms? Will London perhaps persuade Bolshevism to stop at the English Channel? I have already said that Bolshevism has its foreign legions in the form of communist parties in every democratic nation. None of these states can think it is immune to domestic Bolshevism. In a recent by-election for the House of Commons, the independent, that is communist, candidate got 10,000 of the 22,000 votes cast. This was in a district that had formerly been a conservative stronghold. That means that within a short time, the parties to the right lost nearly half of their voters in this district to the communists.

That is proof that the Bolshevist danger exists in England too, and that it will not go away simply because it is ignored.

We place no faith in any territorial promises that the Soviet Union may make. Bolshevism draws ideological as well as military boundaries, which poses a danger to every nation. The world no longer has the choice between falling back into its old fragmentation or accepting a new order for Europe under Axis leadership. The only choice now is between living under Axis military protection or in a Bolshevist Europe.

I am firmly convinced that the lamenting lords and archbishop in London have not the slightest intention of resisting the Bolshevist danger that would result were the Soviet army to enter Europe. Jewry has so deeply infected the Anglo-Saxon states both spiritually and politically that they no longer have the ability to see or accept the danger. It conceals itself as Bolshevism in the Soviet Union, and plutocratic-capitalism in the Anglo-Saxon states. The Jewish race has always been an expert at mimicry, that is, the systematic ability to fade into its surroundings. We know that from our own past. This mimicry puts the host peoples to sleep; it drugs them, paralyzing their ability to defend themselves against the acute and life-threatening danger from Jewry.

Our insight into the matter led us to the early realization that cooperation between international plutocracy and international Bolshevism was not the contradiction it first seems to be, but rather a sign of deep commonalities. The hand of the pseudo-civilized Jewry of Western Europe shakes the hand of the Jewry of the Eastern ghettos over Germany. Europe is in deadly danger [, even if the English do not want to admit it].

I do not, of course, flatter myself into believing that my remarks will influence public opinion in neutral, much less the enemy, states. That is also not my goal. I have no wish to do so [, for I am speaking to the German people, not to the world]. I know that, given our problems on the Eastern Front, the English press tomorrow will furiously attack me with the accusation that I have made the first peace feelers. That is certainly not so. No one in Germany thinks today of a cowardly compromise. The entire people thinks only of a hard war! As a spokesman for the leading nation of the continent, however, I claim the right to call a danger a danger if it threatens not only our own land, but also our entire continent! We National Socialists have the duty to sound the alarm against International Jewry's attempt to plunge the European continent into chaos, and to warn that Jewry has in Bolshevism a terrorist military power whose danger cannot be overestimated.

My third thesis is that the danger is immediate. The spiritual paralysis of the Western European democracies before their deadliest threat is frightening. International Jewry is doing all it can to encourage such paralysis. During our struggle for power in Germany, Jewish newspapers tried to conceal the danger, until the National Socialist movement awakened the people. It is just the same today with other peoples. Jewry once again reveals itself as the incarnation of evil, as the plastic demon of decay, and as the bearer of international culture-destroying chaos.

This explains, by the way, our consistent Jewish policies [, even when the Jews can still call out their old guard of supporters in Berlin]. We see Jewry as a direct threat to every nation. We do not care what other peoples do about the danger. What we do to defend ourselves is our own business, however, and we will not tolerate objections from others. Jewry is a contagious infection. Enemy nations may raise hypocritical protests against our measures against Jewry and cry crocodile tears, but that will not stop us from doing that which is necessary. Germany, in any event, has no intention of bowing before this Jewish threat, but rather intends to act at the right moment, using if necessary the most total and radical measures to [extermin-, to] deal with Jewry.

The military challenges of the Reich in the East are at the center of everything. The war of mechanized robots against Germany and Europe has reached its high point. In resisting the grave and direct threat with its weapons, the German people and its Axis allies are fulfilling in the truest sense of the word a European mission. Our courageous and just battle against this worldwide plague will not be hindered by the worldwide outcry of International Jewry. It can and must end only with victory!

The battle of Stalingrad is a symbol of heroic, manly resistance to the revolt of the steppes. It has not only a military, but also a deep intellectual and spiritual significance for the German people. Here for the first time our eyes have been opened to the true nature of the war. We want no more false hopes and illusions. We want to look the facts bravely in the face, however hard and dreadful they may be. The history of our party and our state has proven that a danger recognized is a danger half defeated. Our coming hard battles in the East will be under the sign of this heroic resistance. It will require efforts by our soldiers and our weapons undreamed of in all their previous campaigns. A merciless war is raging in the East. The Führer was right when he said, in his proclamation of 30 January, that in the end there will not be winners and losers, only those who survive and those who are destroyed.

The German people has recognized that clearly. Its healthy instincts have led it through the war's daily confusion of intellectual and spiritual difficulties. We know today that the Blitzkrieg in Poland and the campaign in the West have only limited significance compared to the battle in the East. The German nation is fighting for everything that it has. We know that the German people is defending its holiest possessions: its families, its women, and its children, its beautiful and untouched countryside, its cities and villages, its two-thousand-year-old culture, everything, indeed, that makes life worth living.

Bolshevism of course has not the slightest appreciation for our nation's treasures, and would take no heed of them whatsoever if it came to that. It did not do so even for its own people. The Soviet Union over the last twenty-five years built up Bolshevism's military potential to an unimaginable degree, and one we falsely evaluated. Terrorist Jewry had two hundred million people to serve it in Russia. It cynically used its methods to create out of the stolid toughness of the Russian people a grave danger for the civilized nations of Europe. A whole nation in the East was driven to battle. Men, women, and even children are employed not only in armaments factories, but in the war itself. Two hundred million live under the terror of the GPU, partially captives of a devilish viewpoint, partially of absolute stupidity. The masses of tanks we have faced on the Eastern Front are the result of twenty-five years of social misfortune and misery on the part of the Bolshevist people. We have to respond with similar measures if we do not want to give up the game as lost.

JOSEPH GOEBBELS

My firm conviction is that we cannot overcome the Bolshevist danger unless we use equivalent, though not identical, methods. The German people faces the gravest demand of the war, namely of finding the determination to use all our resources to protect everything we have and to gain everything we will need in the future. [Today, we can no longer maintain a high standard of living at the cost of our defensive strength in the East. Instead, we must increase our defensive strength at the cost of a high domestic standard of living that is no longer appropriate under the conditions.

That does not mean we are imitating Bolshevist methods. We used different methods earlier in our battle with the Communist Party than we used against the middle-class parties. We faced an opponent who had to be dealt with differently. It used terror to fight the National Socialist movement. Terror is countered not with intellectual arguments, but rather only with counter-terror!

Bolshevism's intellectual threat is well known. Those abroad do not dispute it. But we, and Europe, now face a direct military threat that goes beyond the intellectual threat. To respond to it only with intellectual arguments would probably give those in power in the Kremlin good cause to laugh. We are not so stupid or shortsighted as to even attempt to fight Bolshevism with such unsuitable methods. Nor are we willing, as the proverb has it, to choose our own butcher. We are determined to defend our lives with all the strength we have, not caring whether or not the rest of the world sees the need for this battle.]

Total war is the demand of the hour! We must put an end to the bourgeois attitude that we have also seen in this war: Wash my back, but don't get me wet! The danger facing us is enormous. The efforts we take to meet it must be just as enormous. The time has come to remove the kid gloves and use our fists! We can no longer make only partial and careless use of the rich war potential at home and in the significant parts of Europe that we control. We must use our full resources, as quickly and thoroughly as it is organizationally and practically possible. Unnecessary concern is wholly out of place. The future of Europe hangs on our battle in the East. We are ready to defend it. The German people is shedding its most valuable blood in this battle. The rest of Europe should at least work to support us. Those in the rest of Europe who today do not understand that will thank us tomorrow on bended knees for taking on the task.

It bothers us not in the least that our enemies abroad claim that our total war measures resemble those of Bolshevism. They claim hypocritically that that means there is no need to fight Bolshevism [, since we are Bolshevists ourselves]. The question here is not one of the method one uses to defeat Bolshevism, but of the goal, namely eliminating the danger. The question is not whether the methods we use are good or bad, but whether they are successful. The National Socialist government is ready to use every means. We do not care if anyone objects. We are not willing to weaken Germany's war potential by measures that maintain a high, almost peacetime standard of living for a certain class, thereby endangering our war effort. On the contrary, we are voluntarily giving up a significant part of our living standard to increase our war effort as quickly and completely as possible.

As countless letters from the homeland and the front have shown, by the way, the entire German people agrees. Everyone knows that if we lose, all will be destroyed. The people and leadership are determined to take the most radical measures. The broad working masses of our people are not unhappy because the government is too ruthless. If anything, they are unhappy because it is too considerate. Ask anyone in Germany, and he will say: The most radical is just radical enough, and the most total is just total enough to gain victory!

The total war effort has become a matter of the entire German people. No one has any excuse for ignoring its demands. A storm of applause from the masses greeted my call on 30 January for total war. I can, therefore, assure you that the leadership's measures are in full agreement with the desires of the German people at home and at the front. The people is willing to bear any burden, even the heaviest, to make any sacrifice, if it leads to the great goal of victory.

This naturally assumes that the burdens are shared equally. We cannot tolerate a situation in which most people carry the burden of the war, while a small, passive portion attempts to escape its burdens and responsibilities. The measures we have taken, and will take, will be characterized by the spirit of National Socialist justice. We pay no heed to class or occupation. Rich and poor, high and low must share the burdens equally. Everyone must do his duty in this grave hour, whether by choice or otherwise. We know this has the full support of the people. We would rather do too much rather than too little to achieve victory. No war in history has ever been lost because the leadership had too many soldiers. Many, however, have been lost because the opposite was true.

[I have already told the public that the critical task of the moment is to provide the Führer, through the measures we take at home, with the operative reserves he will need for the longed-for offensives of the coming spring and summer! The more we give the Führer, the more deadly that blow will be! It is no longer appropriate to dream of peace—the German people must think only of the war. That will not prolong the war, but rather shorten it: the most total and most radical war is also the shortest.

We must take the offensive once again in the East. We have the necessary resources. We must mobilize them, and not only in an organized and bureaucratic manner, but also we must improvise. Following bureaucratic channels takes too long! Time is short! We most move quickly! In the National Socialist movement's earlier struggle against the democratic state, we did not always follow a careful plan. We often lived from hand to mouth, following a political strategy of improvisation. That must again become the case. It is time to get the slackers moving! They must be shaken out of their comfortable ease. We cannot wait until they come to their senses. That might be too late. The alarm must sound throughout the nation.] Millions of hands must get to work throughout the country.

We know that the measures we have taken, and the ones we must still take, and which I shall discuss later in this speech, are critical for our whole public and private life. The individual may have to make great sacrifices, but they are tiny when compared to the sacrifices he would have to make if his refusal brought down on us the greatest national disaster. It is better to operate at the right time than to wait until the disease has taken root. One may not complain to the doctor or sue him for bodily injury. He cuts not to kill, but to save the patient's life.

Again let me say that the heavier the sacrifices the German people must make, the more urgent it is that they be fairly shared. The people want it that way. No one resists even the heaviest burdens of war. But it angers people when a few always try to escape the burdens. The National Socialist government has both the moral and political duty to oppose such attempts with strength and determination, if necessary with draconic penalties. Leniency here would be completely out of place, leading in time to confusion in the people's emotions and attitudes that would be a grave danger to our public morale.

We are therefore compelled to adopt a series of measures that are not essential for the war effort in themselves, but seem necessary to maintain moral at home and at the front. The optics of the war, that is, how things outwardly appear, is of decisive importance in this fourth year of war. In view of the superhuman sacrifices that the front makes each day, it has a basic right to expect that no one at home claims the right to ignore the war and its demands. And not only the front demands this, but also the overwhelming, decent population of the homeland. The industrious have a right to expect that if they work ten or twelve or fourteen hours a day, a lazy person does not stand next to them who thinks them foolish, not very clever. The homeland must stay pure and intact in its entirety. Nothing may disturb the picture.

There are, therefore, a series of measures that take account of the war's optics. We have ordered, for example, the closing of bars and nightclubs. I cannot imagine that people who are doing their duty for the war effort still have the energy to stay out late into the night in such places. I can only conclude that they are not taking their responsibilities seriously. We have closed these establishments because they began to offend us, and because they disturbed the image of the war. [The German people will not stand for that.] We have nothing against these amusements as such. After the war we will happily go by the rule "Live and let live." But during a war, the slogan must be "Fight and let fight!"

We have also closed luxury restaurants that demand far more resources than is reasonable. It may be that an occasional person thinks that, even during war, his stomach is the most important thing. We cannot pay him any heed. At the front everyone from the simple soldier to the general field marshal eats from the field kitchen. I do not believe that it is asking too much to insist that we in the homeland pay heed to at least the basic laws of community thinking. We can become gourmets once again when the war is over. Right now, we have more important things to do than worry about our stomachs.

Countless luxury stores have also been closed. They often offended the buying public. There was generally nothing to buy, unless perhaps one paid here and there with butter or eggs instead of money. What good do shops do that no longer have anything to sell, but only use electricity, heating, and human labor that is lacking everywhere else, particularly in the armaments industry.

It is no excuse to say that keeping some of these shops open impresses foreigners. Foreigners will be impressed only by victory! [During the struggle for power, we were poor Nazis! Once we won, everyone wanted to be our friend.] Everyone will want to be our friend if we win the war, too. But if we lose, we will probably be able to count our friends on the fingers of one hand.

We have put an end to such illusions that disturb the war's appearance. We want to put these people standing in empty shops to useful work in the war economy. This process is already in motion, and will be completed by 15 March. Hundreds of thousands of people will be affected. It is, of course, a major transformation of our entire economic life. We are following a plan; we are not, of course, nervous about things. We do not want to accuse anyone unjustly or open them to complaints and accusations from every side. We are only doing what is necessary. But we are doing it quickly and thoroughly. We would rather wear mended clothing for a few years than have our people wear rags for a few centuries.

What good, for example, are fashion salons today? They only use light, heat, and workers. They will reappear when the war is over, when we once again have the time and desire for them. What good are beauty shops that encourage a cult of beauty and take enormous time and energy? In peace they are wonderful, but useless during war. [Our women and girls do not need to worry.] Our women and girls will be able to greet our victorious returning soldiers even without their peacetime finery.

Government offices will work faster and less bureaucratically. It does not leave a good impression when [the folders are put away and] the office closes on the dot after eight hours. The people are not there for the offices; the offices are there for the people. One [does not work until the clock strikes, but rather one] works until the work is done. That is a requirement of the war. If the Führer can do that, so can his paid employees. If there is not enough work to fill the extended hours, 10 or 20 or 30 percent of the workers can be transferred to war production and replace other men for service at the front. That is what has to be done!

That is true for every office at home, both civilian and military. That by itself may make the work in some offices go more quickly and easily. We must learn from the war to operate quickly, not only thoroughly. The soldier at the front does not have weeks to think things over, to pass his thoughts up the line or let them sit in dusty files. He must act immediately or lose his life. In the homeland we do not lose our lives if we work slowly, but we do endanger the survival of the Reich.

[Senseless work in industry and administration that has nothing to do with the war must also be stopped. Things that are fine and worthy during peace can be ridiculous, at the least, during war. For example, I have heard that a variety of offices in Berlin spent weeks discussing whether the word *Akkumulator* should be replaced by the word *Sammler*. Thick files resulted. It seems to me, and I believe that the German people agrees with me, that people who spend their time on such foolishness during the war are not fully employed, and might better be sent to an armaments factory or to the front!

Those who work for the people must constantly provide the people with a good example in everything that they do. Trivial matters can sometimes cause public distress. For example, it is upsetting when young men and women ride horses through the Tiergarten in Berlin at 9:00 A.M. in the morning. They might meet a working woman returning from a ten-hour night shift, who is perhaps going home to take care of three or four or five children. The sight of a cavalcade of horses passing by, as if it were peacetime, can only make this fine working woman's soul bitter. I have, therefore, banned horseback riding on all public streets and parks

JOSEPH GOEBBELS

in the Reich capital for the duration of the war. I believe that, in so doing, I am taking heed of the war's psychological demands, and paying proper consideration for the front. A soldier on leave in Berlin for a few days from the Eastern Front, for example, who sees such a sight will have an entirely false impression of our Reich capital. He does not see the armaments factories, where hundreds of thousands of decent, hardworking people labor for twelve, fourteen, and sometimes sixteen hours a day, but rather a cheerful, lazy riding club. What kind of picture of the homeland will he take back with him to the front!]

Everyone must learn to heed war morale, and pay attention to the just demands of working and fighting people. We are not spoilsports, but neither will we tolerate those who hinder our efforts.

It is, for example, intolerable that certain men and women lounge around for weeks in spas and trade rumors, taking places away from wounded soldiers or from workers who are entitled to a vacation after a year [or two] of hard work. That is intolerable, and we have put an end to it. The war is not a time for amusement. Until it is over, we take our deepest satisfaction in work and battle. Those who do not understand that by themselves must be taught to understand it, and forced if need be. The harshest measures may be needed.

It does not look good, for example, when we devote enormous propaganda to the theme: "Wheels must roll for victory!" with the result that people avoid unnecessary travel only to see unemployed pleasure-seekers find more room for themselves in the trains. The railroad serves to transport war goods and travelers on war business. Only those who need a rest from hard work deserve a vacation. The Führer has not had a day of vacation since the war began, or long before that. Since the first man of the country takes his duty so seriously and responsibly, it must be a silent, yet unmistakable, expectation for every citizen.

On the other hand, the government is doing all it can to give working people the relaxation they need in these trying times. Theaters, movie houses, and music halls remain in full operation. The radio is working to expand and improve its programming. We have no intention of inflicting a gray winter mood on our people.

That which serves the people and keeps up their fighting and working strength is good and essential to the war effort. We want to eliminate the opposite. To balance the measures I have already discussed, I [, in cooperation with party comrade Ley,] have therefore ordered that cultural and intellectual establishments that serve the people not be decreased, but rather increased.

That applies to sports as well. Sports are not only for favored circles today. Military exemptions for athletes are out of place. The purpose of sports is to steel the body, with the goal of using it appropriately in time of the people's greatest need.

The front shares our desires. It demands solidarity with the entire German people in the homeland. We can no longer tolerate efforts that only waste time and resources. We will waste no more time and energy on them. We will not put up with complicated questionnaires on every possible issue. We do not want to worry about a thousand minor matters that may have been important in peace, but are entirely unimportant during war.

We know what we have to do. The German people wants everyone, high and low, rich and poor, to share a Spartan lifestyle. The Führer gives us all an example, one that must be followed by everyone. He knows only work and care. We do not want to leave it all to him, but rather we want to take that part of it from him that we are able to bear.

The present day has a remarkable resemblance for every genuine National Socialist to the period of struggle. We have always acted in the same way. We were with the people through thick and thin, and that is why the people followed us. We have always carried our burdens together with the people, and therefore they did not seem heavy to us, but rather light. The people wants to be led. Never in history have the people failed a brave and determined leadership at a critical hour.

Let me say a few words in this regard about practical measures in our total war effort that we have already taken. The problem is freeing soldiers for the front, and freeing workers for the armaments industry. These are the primary goals, even at the cost of our living standard during the war. This does not mean a permanent decline in our standard of living. It is only a means to an end.

JOSEPH GOEBBELS

As part of this campaign, hundreds of thousands of military exemptions must be eliminated. These exemptions were given because we did not have enough skilled labor to fill the positions that would have been left open by revoking them. The reason for our current measures, and the ones to come, is to mobilize the necessary workers. That is why we have appealed to men not working in the war economy, and to women who were not working at all. They will not and cannot ignore our call. The duty for women to work is broad. That does not, however, mean that only those included in the law have to work. Anyone is welcome. The more who join the war effort, the more soldiers we can free for the front [, and the harder the Führer will be able to strike in the coming summer].

Our enemies maintain that German women are not able to replace men in the war economy. That may be true for certain fields of heavy labor. But I am convinced that the German woman is determined to fill the spot left by the man leaving for the front, and to do so as soon as possible, and fully! We do not need to point to Bolshevism's example. For years, millions of the best German women have been working successfully in war production, and they wait impatiently to be joined and assisted by others as soon as possible. All those who join in the work are only giving the proper thanks to those at the front. Hundreds of thousands have already joined, and hundreds of thousands more will join. We hope soon to free up armies of workers, who will in turn free up armies of fighting soldiers.

I would think little of German women if I believed that they do not want to listen to my appeal. They will not seek to follow the letter of the law, or to slip through its loopholes. [I do not believe that. I cannot imagine it.] The few who may try will not succeed. We will not accept a doctor's excuse. Nor will we accept the alibi that one must help one's husband or relative or good friend as a way of avoiding work. We will respond appropriately. The few who may attempt it will only lose the respect of those around them. [We will not forget them; we will remember them after the war is over.] The people will despise them.

No one expects a woman lacking the requisite physical strength to go to work in a tank factory. There are, however, numerous jobs in war production that do not demand great physical strength, and that a woman can do even if she comes from the better circles. No one is too good to work, and we all have only the choice to give up what we have, or to lose everything.

It is also time to ask women with household help if they really need it. One can take care of the house and children oneself, freeing the servant for other tasks, or leave the house and children in care of the servant or the NSV,[3] and go to work oneself. Life may not be as pleasant as it is during peace. [When Daddy comes home, Mommy may not have supper ready.] But we are not at peace, we are at war. We can be comfortable after we have won the war. Now we must sacrifice our comforts to gain victory.

Soldiers' wives surely understand this. They know it is their duty to their husbands to support them by doing work that is important to the war effort. That is true above all in agriculture. The wives of farmers have set a good example. Both men and women must be sure that no one does less during war than they did in peace; more work must instead be done in every area.

One may not, by the way, make the mistake of leaving everything to the government. The government can only set the broad guidelines. To give life to those guidelines is the job of working people, under the inspiring leadership of the party. Fast action is essential. One must go beyond the legal requirements. "Volunteer!" is the slogan.

As *Gauleiter* of Berlin, I appeal above all to my fellow Berliners. They have given enough good examples of noble behavior and bravery during the war such that they will not fail here. Their practical behavior and good cheer even during war have earned them a good name throughout the world. This good name must be maintained and strengthened! If I appeal to my fellow Berliners to do some important work quickly, thoroughly, and without complaint, I know they will all obey. We do not want to complain about the difficulties of the day or grump to one another. Rather we want to behave not only like Berliners, but also like Germans, by getting to work, acting, seizing the initiative and doing something, not leaving it to someone else.

What German woman would want to ignore my appeal on behalf of those fighting at the front? Who would want to put personal

JOSEPH GOEBBELS

comfort above national duty? Who in view of the serious threat we face would want to consider his egotistic private needs instead of the requirements of the war that come before everything else?

I reject with contempt the enemy's claim that we are imitating Bolshevism. We do not want to imitate Bolshevism; we want to defeat it, with whatever means are necessary, just as we did during the period of struggle. The German woman will best understand what I mean, for she has long known that the war our men are fighting today above all is a war to protect her children. Her holiest possession is guarded by our people's most valuable blood. The German woman must spontaneously proclaim her solidarity with the fighting men. She had better join the ranks of millions of workers in the homeland's army, and do it tomorrow rather than the day after tomorrow, adding herself to the army of the working homeland. A river of readiness must flow through the German people. I expect that countless women, and above all men, who are not doing essential war work will report to the authorities. He who gives quickly gives twice as much.

Our general economy is consolidating [, as has already been reported by the press]. I know that many of our people are making great sacrifices. We understand their sacrifices, and the government is trying to keep them to the necessary minimum. But some must remain, and must unfortunately be borne. When the war is over, we will build up that which we now are eliminating, more generously and more beautifully, and the state will lend its hand.

I energetically reject the charge that our measures will eliminate the middle class or result in a monopoly economy. The middle class will immediately regain its economic and social position after the war. The current measures are necessary for the war effort. They aim not at a structural transformation of the economy, but merely at gaining total victory.

I do not dispute the fact that these measures will cause problems in the coming weeks. They will, however, give us breathing room. We are laying the groundwork for the actions of the coming summer, without paying any heed to the threats and boasting of the enemy. I am happy to reveal this plan for victory to the German people. It not only accepts these measures, it has demanded them, demanded them more strongly than ever before during the war. The people wants comprehensive and rapid action! It is time for it! We must use our time to prepare for coming surprises.

In past years, we have often recalled the example of Frederick the Great in newspapers and in speeches. We really did not have the right to do so. For a while during the Third Silesian War, Frederick II had five million Prussians, according to Schlieffen, standing against 90,000,000 enemies. In the second of seven hellish years he suffered a defeat that shook Prussia's foundations. He never had enough soldiers, never enough weapons, to fight without risking everything. His strategy was always one of improvisation. His principle was to attack the enemy whenever it was possible, to engage him whenever he met him. He suffered defeats, but that was not decisive. What was decisive is that the Great King remained unbroken, that he was unshaken by the changing fortunes of war, that his strong heart overcame every danger. At the end of seven years of war, he was fifty-one years old. He had no teeth, he suffered from gout, and was tortured by a thousand pains, but he stood above the devastated battlefield as the victor.

How can we compare our situation with his? Let us show the same will and decisiveness as he, and when the time comes do as he did, remaining unshakable through all the twists of fate, and like him win the battle even under the most unfavorable circumstances. Let us never doubt the great cause we are fighting for.

I am firmly convinced that the German people has been deeply moved by the blow of fate at Stalingrad. It has looked into the face of hard and pitiless war. It knows the terrible truth. [It is resolved to follow the Führer through thick and thin. We have brave and loyal allies at our side. The Italian people, under the leadership of their great Ducé, will follow us on the path to victory. Fascist doctrine has prepared them for great trials of fate. In East Asia, the brave Japanese people are striking blow after blow against Anglo-Saxon military forces. Three great world powers, together with their allies, are battling plutocratic tyranny. What can befall us if we meet the hard trials of this war with firm determination? There is no doubt about the certainty of our victory!

JOSEPH GOEBBELS

While our front in the East is fighting a gigantic defensive battle against the assault of the steppes, our submarines are waging war on the world's oceans. Enemy shipping is suffering losses that can in no way be replaced, no matter how great their efforts to refit old ships or build new ones. And in the coming summer, the enemy will become reacquainted with our offensive power! The German people is determined to use all its energies to provide the Führer with the necessary resources to accomplish that. That is the task of the hour!

I am nearing my conclusion.] The English and American press in recent days has been writing at length about the attitude of the German people during this crisis. The English seem to think that they know the German people much better than we do, its own leadership. They give hypocritical advice on what we should do and not do. They believe that the German people today is the same as the German people of November 1918 that fell victim to their persuasive wiles. I do not need to disprove their assertions. That will come each day from the German people.

To make the truth plain, however, my German people's comrades, I want to ask you a series of questions. I want you to answer them to the best of your knowledge, according to your conscience. When my audience spontaneously cheered on 30 January, the English [-American—in other words, the Jewish] press reported the next day that it was all a propaganda show that did not represent the true opinion of the German people [, which the Jews know better than we do].

I have invited to today's meeting a cross section of the whole German people in the best sense of the word. In front of me are rows of wounded German soldiers from the Eastern Front, missing legs and arms, with wounded bodies, those who have lost their sight, those who have come with nurses, men in the blush of youth who stand with crutches. Among them are fifty who bear the Knight's Cross with Oak Leaves, shining examples of our fighting front. Behind them are armaments workers from Berlin tank factories. Behind them are party officials, soldiers from the fighting army, doctors, scientists, artists, engineers and architects, teachers, officials and employees from offices, proud representatives of every area of our intellectual life that even in the midst of war produce miracles of human invention and genius. Throughout the Sport Palace I see thousands of German women. The youth are here, as are the aged. No class, no occupation, no age remained uninvited. I can rightly say that before me is gathered a representative sample of the whole German people, both from the front and the homeland. Is that true? Yes or no? [Well, the Jews are not represented here!]

You, my hearers, at this moment represent the whole nation to the world. I wish to ask you ten questions that you will answer for the German people throughout the world, but especially for our enemies, who are listening to us on the radio. Are you willing?

The English maintain that the German people has lost faith in victory.

I ask you: Do you believe with the Führer and us in the final total victory of German weapons? I ask you: Are you resolved to follow the Führer through thick and thin to victory, and are you willing to accept the heaviest personal burdens?

Second, the English say that the German people is tired of fighting.

I ask you: Are you ready to follow the Führer as the phalanx of the homeland, standing behind the fighting army, and to wage war with wild determination through all the turns of fate until victory is ours?

Third: The English maintain that the German people has no desire any longer to accept the government's growing demands for war work.

I ask you: Soldiers and workers, are you and the German people willing to work, if the Führer orders, ten, twelve, and if necessary fourteen or sixteen hours a day, and to give your all for victory?

Fourth: The English maintain that the German people is resisting the government's total war measures. It does not want total war, the English say, but rather capitulation!

I ask you: Do you want total war? If necessary, do you want a war more total and radical than anything that we can even imagine today?

Fifth: The English maintain that the German people has lost faith in the Führer.

I ask you: [Do you trust the Führer?] Is your confidence in the

Führer greater, more faithful, and more unshakable than ever before? Are you absolutely and completely ready to follow him wherever he goes and do all that is necessary to bring the war to a victorious end?

Sixth, I ask you: Are you ready from now on to give your full strength to provide [our fighting fathers and brothers on] the Eastern Front with the men and munitions needed to defeat Bolshevism? [Are you prepared to do that?]

Seventh, I ask you: Do you take a holy oath to the front that the homeland stands firm and unshakable behind them, and that you will give them everything they need to win the victory?

Eighth, I ask you: Do you, especially you women, want the government to do all it can to encourage German women to put their full strength at work to support the war effort, and to release men for the front whenever possible? [Is that what you want?]

Ninth, I ask you: Do you approve, if necessary, the most radical measures against a small group of shirkers and black marketers who pretend there is peace in the middle of war and exploit the needs of the people for their own selfish purposes? Do you agree that those who harm the war effort should lose their heads?

Tenth and lastly, I ask you: Do you agree that above all in war, according to the National Socialist party platform, the same rights and duties should apply to all, that the homeland should bear the heavy burdens of the war together, and that the burdens should be shared equally between high and low and rich and poor? [Is that what you want?]

I have asked; you have given me your answers. You are part of the people, and your answers are those of the German people. You have told our enemies what they needed to hear so that they will have no illusions or false ideas.

Now, just as in the first hours of our rule and through the ten years that followed, we are bound firmly in brotherhood with the German people. The most powerful ally on earth, the people itself, stands behind us and is determined to follow the Führer, come what may. It will accept the heaviest burdens to gain victory.

I stand before you not only as the spokesman of the government, but as the spokesman of the people. My old party friends are around me here, clothed with the high offices of the people and the government. Party comrade Speer sits next to me. The Führer has given him the great task of mobilizing the German armaments industry and supplying the front with all the weapons it needs. Party comrade Dr. Ley sits next to me. The Führer has charged him with the leadership of the German workforce, with schooling and training them in untiring work for the war effort. We feel deeply indebted to our party comrade Sauckel, who has been charged by the Führer to bring countless hundreds of thousands of workers to the Reich to support our national economy. All the leaders of the party, the military, and government join with us as well.

We are all children of our people, forged together in this most critical hour of our national history. We swear to you, we swear to the front, we swear to the Führer, that we will together mold the homeland into a force on which the Führer and his fighting soldiers can rely on absolutely and blindly. We promise to do all in our life and work that is necessary for victory. We will fill our hearts with the political passion, with the ever-burning fire, that blazed during the great struggles of the party and the state. Never during this war will we fall prey to the false and hypocritical objectivism that has brought the German nation so much misfortune over its history.

When the war began, we turned our eyes to the nation alone. That which serves its struggle for life is good and must be maintained and encouraged. What harms its struggle for life is bad and must be eliminated and cut out. With burning hearts and cool heads we will overcome the major problems of this phase of the war. We are on the way to eventual victory. That victory rests on our faith in the Führer. He expects us to do that which will throw all we have done before into the shadows. We do not want to fail him. As we are proud of him, he should be proud of us.

The great crises and upsets of national life show who the true men, and also the true women, are. We have no right any longer to speak of the weaker sex, for both sexes are displaying the same determination and passionate spiritual strength. The nation is ready for anything. The Führer has commanded, and we will follow him!

JOSEPH GOEBBELS

If ever we have loyally and unshakably believed in victory, it is in this hour of national reflection and contemplation. We see it before us; we need only reach for it. We must resolve to subordinate everything to it. That is the duty of the hour. Let the slogan be:

People, rise up, and storm, break loose![4]

NOTES

1. Albert Speer, *Inside the Third Reich* (New York: Simon & Schuster, 1970), 257.

2. The source is a recording of the speech titled "Kundgebung der NSDAP, Gau Berlin, im Berliner Sportpalast: Proklamation des totalen Krieges," *Deutsches Rundfunkarchiv* (Wiesbaden), Nr. 260052.

3. The NSV was the Nazi Party's charity branch.

4. This is a well-known line from a poem by Theodor Körner (1791–1813). Goebbels also cites it in his 1932 speech on p. 37.

Model Speeches for Nazi Leaders: 1944–45

So far, the speeches in this book were delivered by major Nazi leaders to large audiences. There were many more speeches that had a more limited audience. On a national holiday, such as the anniversary of the Nazi takeover on 30 January 1933 or Hitler's birthday on 20 April, each party local group (there were over 20,000 in 1939) was expected to hold a meeting. A local party leader typically gave a speech. The audiences ranged from a handful to the hundreds, but the vast number of such meetings resulted in a huge rhetorical output.

Since the speaking abilities of local Nazi leaders varied greatly, the party provided rhetorical first aid in the form of advice and model speeches. All leaders at the lower level received a monthly journal titled *Die neue Gemeinschaft* ("The New Community"), which gave model programs and speeches for all sorts of occasions. These model speeches were not intended to be read verbatim—although they often were. A 1943 confidential German morale report claimed that the party officials who conducted these meetings found the supporting material indispensable. The following three sample speeches, then, were delivered thousands of times with varying degrees of skill and originality.[1]

The first is a model speech for Mother's Day, 1944. This was a major date on the Nazi calendar. Mothers with four or more children even received medals. The speech emphasizes Nazism's view of women—but also notes that, under the demands of the war, they have had to take on new roles under difficult conditions. The message reinforced the Nazi argument that the war involved everyone, whether at the front or at home.

The second speech deals with a particularly difficult situation: what to say at a mass funeral for those killed in Allied bombing raids. In all, over 500,000 German civilians were killed by Allied bombing during World War II, most of them after 1942. Party leaders tried to give meaning to the deaths, suggesting that civilians, too, were fighting for Germany—and hinting that the Allies would suffer equivalent pain once the "miracle weapons" went into action.

The final model speech was intended for "Duty of Youth Day," on 25 March 1945, a national holiday that marked a rite of passage for fourteen-year-olds. Some would go into vocational training, others to further schooling. It was also the age at which young people were confirmed either in the Protestant or Catholic Church. The speech holds up soldiers as the models for German youth. They are to be ready to die at the Führer's orders, but are also assured that Germany will win the war, and that they will join in the great reconstruction that will follow. By the time these speeches were delivered, the war had little more than a month to run, and even most party officials who delivered them surely knew that Germany would lose.

SAMPLE SPEECH FOR A PARTY LEADER ON MOTHER'S DAY 1944

Dear women and mothers!

We live in a hard, manly age. War has raged for five years, and wars are always fought by men. While girls learn how to use household utensils, it has always been the right and duty of young men to learn how to use weapons, and they have always been proud when they could take them in their hands to defend home and family, to fight for their people. Today is the age of weapons. Every day, we see trains with tanks, artillery, and munitions rolling through our railroad stations to the front, where your husbands, brothers, and sons ceaselessly stand watch, day and night, in rain and sunshine, heat and cold. They have advanced and withdrawn, attacked and defended. They have had sleepless nights, suffered hunger and thirst, endured stress and depravation, along with homesickness and worry about their families at home. They have been wounded, and seen their comrades fall beside them. Weary though they were, danger or orders have roused them again and again, attacking once more or defending against a charging enemy. All this they do for us.

In such a manly age of deeds of arms, it is right to praise and honor the man, the fighter. Many of our soldiers bear the marks of their bravery, their wounds, in the medals they wear. Every day, reports from the front tell the homeland of the deeds and achievements of the men in the field. The newsreels show us pictures of fighting men with lined faces, marked by hardship und privation. When one of them comes home on leave, we do all we can to make these days into real holidays.

Still, the man who fights in the war and risks his life at the front knows that the same honor due to him is also due to women and mothers. How often during quiet moments do soldiers sit in their bunkers or barracks and talk of home. They say: Things here may be bad, but our mothers back home have it even worse than we do, for they are always worrying about us. How true that is. While the men in the field fight with their weapons, women and mothers at home fight with their hearts, bearing the misery and sorrow of their soldiers themselves, showing in difficult hours the same courage and the same loyalty that they do.

Today, on the day of Germany's mothers, to which National Socialism first gave deep meaning, today, women and mothers, we want to express the thanks we have for you, a thanks we feel not only on this day. When children are at home, always with their mother, they know nothing of thankfulness. Mothers cook food and make beds, they darn socks or mend clothing, they help with homework or prepare for a holiday, they sit all night beside a sick child. To children, it all seems normal. How could things be any different? Only when children leave home do they realize how much they miss their mothers, only then do they appreciate and understand what their mothers mean to them. Then a longing for their mothers grows within them, and with the longing comes thanks for all their mothers did, and continue to do. A mother usually does no great deeds, visible from afar: quietly and inconspicuously, she does her duty, which never ends as long as she lives. She wants no reward but that her children are happy and healthy, and grow up to be decent people.

That is why the German people thank their mothers today. Alongside their normal burdens, and aside from their concern about husbands or sons in the field, they have so many other burdens to carry, burdens that demand not only a strong arm, but also a strong heart. They must do the work alone at home and in the yard that they once had help with. Many must work in plants and factories to replace the men in the field, building the weapons they need to fight with. These are difficult challenges, for the woman is the soul of the home, the guardian of the family. This war involves everything. It is waged not only at the front, but also in the homeland. Families are torn apart. Older sons are with the troops, and the husband is often working in some distant part of the Reich. The older daughters are working with the Labor Service or as volunteers. Younger children are sent to camps in the countryside to protect them from terror attacks, no longer cared for by their mothers. Even when a mother knows that her children are well cared for there, and safer than they would be at home, it is hard for her to send them away, to be separated from them. These are all burdens that women in previous centuries did not experience during wars. Today, mothers bear misery and sorrow, and many have paid the heaviest price, sacrificing someone they loved for our fatherland. Their faces have grown hard and lined, but they do not collapse under their toil and concerns, but rather they grow even stronger, always having the strength to use what little they have to bring pleasure to their families. A man is strong through what he does. A woman is strong through her ability to bear suffering, winning thereby blessings for herself and her family. That is why, in the midst of this manly age, the German people praises and honors its mothers, who, just as its soldiers, are enduring the war and helping to win it.

Once more, as in past years, the Führer has awarded some of you the Mother's Cross. I know that a mother who brings children into the world and raises them does not want to be praised or decorated. She sees her motherhood as a gift of God. Some women who hoped in vain for children are envious, for children born in pain and raised through hard work are the greatest, purest joy of a healthy woman. But these children are, at the same time, the joy and future of a people. A people can have the bravest military achievements and create the greatest artistic masterpieces, but it will vanish if its mothers do not assure its survival by bearing children. That is why the Führer decorates women with many children, just as he decorates the bravest soldiers: the German people owes its survival and future to them both. Thus a German mother should and may wear her medal with quiet pride, just as a soldier wears his decorations or medals.

In a time of misery and death, you German mothers have affirmed life, proving your faith in the future of our people. The soldier at the front, through his fighting and sacrifice, protects the cradle. You have ensured that he does not guard empty cradles. While thousands are risking and sacrificing their lives for our people far from home, you have given our people new life, and for that, mothers, all of us owe you our thanks.

Model Speech at a Funeral for Victims of Enemy Bombing, 1944

The men, women, and children who were victims of the malicious air attack have found their final resting place in honored graves in the South Cemetery. We bid farewell to our fellow people's comrades, so suddenly torn from us. Their sacrificial deaths entitle them to rest alongside those who fell in this great war.

Today, we have come together above all to remember those who were the victims of an enemy terror attack during the night of 15 July 1944. When we stand by the grave of a comrade who fell in manly aerial combat, or by the graves of German soldiers who returned with serious injuries from the battle of men at the front, or by the graves of soldiers who bravely fell as they defended us against night attacks, we understand that they gave their lives for Germany in open battle with our enemies. But when we stand alongside the long line of graves of those who died in the bombing terror, when we see and read the names of the dead—here a mother alongside two of her children, while the third cries in the arms of a relative standing by the open grave, there a whole family, or a husband and wife, or over there where a father and daughter lie together in the earth—it reminds us of the criminal nature of our enemies, who wage war against women, children, and old people. The thought burns within us: may our enemies suffer fate's heavy trial far more than we have endured, and still endure.

Some of the dead were close to us: our relatives, or friends. Others we did not know. They came from all parts of the city, from every occupation, from every age group. They all died randomly in the destruction of a night that threatened us all with immediate and hard death. They died. We, too, might have died. As we stand by their graves, we realize once again how all our fates are inseparably connected in this hardest of all wars.

We do not choose our words without thought: A great victory is never won without bitter sacrifice. We must be ready at all times to accept any sacrifice to ensure that our soldiers do not fight in vain. Every hour they stand watch for us, and they will also be victorious in the final battle for the survival of our people. Let us, therefore, be and remain strong!

Our hearts grieve before the graves of those who are now so close to us, who now almost seem to be our brothers and sisters, and our hearts are filled with sympathy for the closest kin. Who would want to try to ease their pain with empty words? Who will close his eyes to the heavy burden each of us carries?

We are being tested. Our conduct in these deadly days shows whether we are loyal, strong, and faithful. A free, proud, and great Germany will not be given to us. Hard battle and hard deprivation prove the value of a person, and of a community.

We have stood by the graves of our dead. They will have died in vain should we prove weak and cowardly. They, too, died for the Reich!

We have looked death in the eye, but we have also seen examples of camaraderie and community that became evident only during the grim nights of bombing.

The song of good comrades[2] is also the song of the unknown heroes of the homeland.

We go back to our lives and to our work. In the future, we will be still braver, still stronger, more loyal, than in the past. This we swear before the dead. The words of the fallen poet Walter Flex live in us:

"You can place full trust only in the dead, who live in you, for there is nothing false in them. Have faith that the best of our people did not die to bring death to the living, but rather that the dead shall come alive!"

MODEL SPEECH FOR DUTY OF YOUTH DAY, MARCH 1945

At the end of the past year, three friends met each other in their hometown after a long separation. Two were home on leave, while the third had been released from military service after a serious injury, and was now working at his trade.

Each of us knows that the end of an old year encourages reflection. We seek a quiet corner to reflect on ourselves and what we have done. We do not think only of the past, but even more we gather the inner strength to find the courage to enter a new year and begin the battle anew. That is what our three friends did. Late one afternoon, they walked the snow-covered path to the ruins of Barbarossa's royal palace, the jewel of their hometown. How often had they played there as children. The faded romance of their childhoods returned. It was only a few years ago, one of them said. These words touched them deeply; they thought about what had become of them since their boyhoods. They met each other in the *Jungvolk*,[3] then became leaders in the Hitler Youth. Since then, their lives had followed duty's law. When they became soldiers, it was only a continuation of the service they had voluntarily done for years. They had not realized how much battle had changed them. Here at Barbarossa's old palace, each realized it for himself. But it was also something that they shared. One of the friends said: "We see these ruins with different eyes now than we did six or seven years ago. In our struggle for the Reich, all the great heroes of centuries past stand with us, wherever we fight.

Memories of our innocent youth are fading, but this is a reminder of peaceful days. It is different for those comrades who come of age in the midst of war, wondering what life has in store for them."

He was talking about you, boys and girls, who will take the oath to the Führer and the flag. The war was already raging on the borders of the fatherland when you joined the German *Jungvolk* or the *Jungmädel*,[4] four years ago. You have been raised under the laws of war. Much happened that you were unable to understand. Now, however, your bodies, minds, and souls are strong enough to take the first step toward independence. Finished with school, you will choose an occupation, and at home and in the Hitler Youth, you will learn to be mature, fighting young Germans.

It is fitting that in the midst of war, we take time to reflect. You would think it wrong if the war, part of our lives both day and night, did not also enter into our hearts. All great deeds come from the heart. Stillness always precedes the storm. Think of the tree that grows from a small seed, or of the fresh greenery appearing in these spring days. None of that would be if the roots were ill. Stillness dwells in the roots. He who heads into battle prepares quietly. He does not make noise about it. But, you say, you are not heading into battle. First, you must battle with life itself. This you must know: Your life is a gift of God through the sacrifice of your mother. She gave birth to you in pain, and as you opened your eyes, she blessed you.

No one knows what the future will bring; the hour at which our lives will end is unknown. The deeds an individual will do are yet unknown. As I look across your ranks and into your eyes, I cannot tell what your fates will be before the boys become soldiers and the girls become mothers. You must choose. But you must know that you control your own fate. It depends on you. God gives the grace necessary for each day—but only to him who is able to master his life. It depends on you. And when you die, those who stand alongside your grave will measure your life by what you have accomplished. Do not misunderstand me. Only a few within a people are fated to do immortal deeds. For some, only their names will endure. But that does not diminish the respect for their lives and achievements.

You are prepared for life, and you now steer your own ship. Each must decide his course. In the first few years, you will surely sail through quiet waters, and you will be surrounded by loving parents, by your friends and comrades. But you will set the course. You must understand what this means. Dear comrades, let us speak of those who bore you, your mothers. You feel as if you are stretching your wings but you would be nothing without your mothers. They do not want to see you as children any longer, though they still wish to protect you, to love you. Now that you are guiding your own course, you should thank them. The mere word is not enough. Love says everything, even without words. Let your mothers tell you today where you come from. Listen to them quietly as they speak of your ancestors, of the old houses in which they were born, of their fields and pastures, of the graves in which they rest. See the letters and the pictures of those who fell as soldiers for the fatherland. And if there are no visible reminders any longer, then open wide your hearts to those of past centuries. You live only because of them. Once more, I speak of the roots that must be there if the tree is to grow and live. Your ancestors are the roots of your lives: honor and respect them. They lived and fought as Germans, ensuring that the original Germans did not perish. God created many peoples, but only one German people.

Were we ever to lose our German nature, our essence, there would be no purpose in living on.

We turn our thoughts to the enemy who wants to destroy us. He does not lust only after our land, our factories, or our buildings. He wants to destroy our inner nature. He wants to take any sense of being German from the youth, so that there will remain only people who can be Germans today, Americans tomorrow, and Englishmen the day after that. In reality, they would be slaves without dignity. Do you understand what the extermination of the German people would mean? That is why you should not live as you wish, but rather you must live above all as a German. I know that you will become decent men and women if you remain true to the laws of our blood. Whenever our history was glorious, there was battle. Often our people stood at the edge of the abyss, but the sun always rose again because our ancestors remained German. I could give name after name. Each name by itself signifies a world of battle and sacrifice. When you have moments of doubt, take strength from the heroes of our history. The stars lit by Armin, Henry I, Ulrich von Hutten, Frederick the Great, and Otto von Bismarck shine through our deepest darkness.

He who speaks to young people of your age in this sixth year of war can speak seriously, for you are all much older than your years. You have brothers at the front. You read their letters, hear their names, speak with enthusiasm of their deeds. There have been times when young people of your age did not need to leave childhood behind them, but we are at war, and you are the last who would seek to escape its demands. Remember that life is never a frenzy of enthusiasm. And inescapable death waits at life's end. Before it takes us, we want to have mastered our lives.

What good fortune it is for each young German to have been born in this age, to be a follower of the Führer. You take an oath to him in this hour. May no one's oath be empty. May each swear from his heart. The Führer needs everyone for the tasks of the war, and then for the peace that will heal all wounds. We do not want to fail, even if our homes are ruined by the enemy's terror and irreplaceable cultural landmarks are destroyed. Let us believe that everything that we lovingly call German will return.

Before you take your oaths, I wish to return to the conversation those three friends had, and with which I began. When you reach their age, you will be different than you are today, and you will have occasion for reflection. May you then be even more firmly German; may your love for the fatherland and your loyalty to the Führer be even stronger. With the will to mature, let your hearts speak:

We are ready!

NOTES

1. The texts are in Johannes Linke, "Beispiel einer Ansprache des Hoheitsträgers zum Muttertag 1944," *Die neue Gemeinschaft* 10 (1944), 169–71; "Gedankenführung der Ansprache für die Opfer des Bombenterrors in der Stadt M. Auch sie starben für das Reich!" *Die neue Gemeinschaft* 10 (1944), 375–76; Alvin Rüffler, "Läßt Eure Herzen sprechen: Wir sind bereit!" *Die neue Gemeinschaft* 11 (1945), 4–7.

2. A well-known German song commemorating those who died in battle.

3. The Nazi organization for boys aged 10–14.

4. The Nazi organization for girls aged 10–14.

Adolf Hitler

Adolf Hitler's Last Speech

30 JANUARY 1945

On 30 January 1933, Hitler became chancellor of Germany. In the twelve years that followed, the anniversary of the Nazi assumption of power was a national holiday. Hitler always gave a speech, broadcast to the nation by radio and printed in full in the newspapers. This speech, delivered on 30 January 1945, was Hitler's final public speech.[1]

The military situation was catastrophic. The Russians were already well into German territory to the east, and England and the United States were charging into Germany from the west, delayed somewhat by the Battle of the Bulge. The promised miracle weapons had proven inadequate. Allied bombers were leveling what was left of major German cities. It was clear to any reasonable observer that Germany had lost the war.

Hitler, however, was unwilling to admit defeat. Instead, he began the speech as he had so many before, with a review of history. He reviewed the Nazi struggle for power before 1933 and the accomplishments of the six years of peace after 1933. His argument used Aristotle's ancient enthymeme of greater versus lesser: because Nazism had been able to overcome Germany's almost hopeless situation in 1933, it would surely succeed in overcoming the lesser challenges of 1945. Hitler stressed the Nazi claim that the human will is stronger than mere numbers or masses of equipment. And he used the standard Nazi argument after the military defeat at Stalingrad in 1943: no matter how bad the situation looked, it would be even worse if Germany lost the war.

Hitler provided his audience with no new reasons to believe that victory was still possible. He simply used what was left of his credibility to tell Germans that he, at least, was convinced that Germany would win, and that he expected all Germans to fight and die, or face a fate even worse than death.

But Hitler's credibility had faded considerably. German internal morale reports showed a surprising boost in morale after Hitler's optimistic New Year address only a month earlier, but that had dissipated quickly, particularly after a major Russian offensive began on 12 January 1945. Now even most loyal Nazis realized that Germany would lose the war. Morale reports found little evidence that this speech restored confidence in victory. That does not mean the speech failed. Germans continued fighting in a hopeless cause for three more months, the war ending only after Hitler committed suicide in the ruins of Berlin.

SPEECH BROADCAST TO THE NATION, 30 JANUARY 1945

Fellow German people's comrades! National Socialists![2]

When the immortal Reich President von Hindenberg charged me twelve years ago, as the leader of the strongest party, with the chancellorship, Germany's internal situation was the same as its current international situation. The Treaty of Versailles along with the democratic republic had instituted a systematic and continued process of economic disruption and destruction. Gradually, a state developed in which it seemed normal to have nearly seven million people permanently unemployed, seven million working only part-time, ruined farmers, a destroyed industrial system, and a standstill in commerce. German harbors were ship cemeteries. Financial collapse threatened not only the national government, but also the provinces and cities.

The decisive factor, however, was this: Behind the methodical destruction of the German economy stood the specter of Asiatic Bolshevism, then as well as today. Just as is the case today, the bourgeois world was entirely unable to effectively resist these developments in the years before our takeover of power.

In the years after the collapse of 1918, people still had not realized that an old world was collapsing and a new one was rising. One could not preserve that which had proved rotten and corrupt, no matter how hard one tried. Rather, it was necessary to build on a new foundation. An outdated social order had collapsed, and any attempt to maintain it would be in vain. It is no different today, though on a larger scale. The bourgeois states are doomed to destruction, and only those people's communities with clear and firm worldviews are in a position to overcome Europe's worst crisis in many centuries.

We had only six years of peace after 30 January 1933. Enormous things happened in those six years. Even greater things were planned, things so great and so impressive that they aroused the envy of the incompetent democratic nations around us. The decisive thing that happened in these six years, however, was that, after enormous exertions, the German national body was remilitarized. This was not primarily a matter of military equipment, but rather a filling of the country with the spiritual will to resist, with the desire for self-assertion.

Terrible things are happening in the East. Tens and hundreds of thousands of people are being exterminated in villages and market towns, in the countryside and in the cities. In the end, our enormous efforts will defend against and master the situation, despite all the setbacks and hard tests. That is possible only because there was an inner transformation of the German people in the years after 1933. If the Germany of the Treaty of Versailles still existed today, Europe would long since have been swept away by the Asiatic flood. One hardly needs say anything to the ever-present fools who think that a defenseless Germany would never have fallen victim to the Jewish international world conspiracy. That would be to ignore all natural laws. Has there ever been a defenseless goose left uneaten by a fox, since her nature makes it impossible for her to have aggressive intentions? And when will the wolf become a pacifist, since the sheep have no weapons? The fact that such bourgeois sheep exist who earnestly believe that is, as I said, proof of how necessary it was to put an end to an era that bred such creatures, that even gave them political influence.

Long before National Socialism came to power, a bitter battle already raged against Jewish-Asiatic Bolshevism. It failed to overrun Europe in the years 1919–1920 only because it was then too weak and unarmed. Its attack on Poland was not given up because of any sympathy for the Poles of the time, but rather because it lost the Battle of Warsaw. The attempt to destroy Hungary failed not because one had second thoughts, but rather because Bolshevist military power could not be sustained. The attempt to ruin Germany was given up not because they no longer wished to do it, but rather because they did not succeed in overcoming our people's last natural powers of resistance. Immediately afterwards, Jewry began systematically to undermine our people, and had its best allies in those thick-headed citizens who did not want to see that the age of the bourgeois world was over and would never return, that the age of unrestrained economic liberalism could lead only to collapse. Above all, they did not realize that the great tasks of the age can be mastered only by an authoritarian government bringing together the strength of the nation, based on the principle that equal rights for all means equal duties for all, and correspondingly, fulfilling these equal duties necessarily must lead to equal rights.

In the midst of its enormous economic, social, and cultural constructive activities, National Socialist education also gave the German people the foundation on which military values depend. Our nation's powers of resistance have grown so enormously since 30 January 1933 that they can no longer be compared with those of the former age. Maintaining this inner strength to resist is the surest guarantee for final victory!

Europe today suffers serious illness. The affected states will either gather their full and utmost powers of resistance to overcome it, or they will perish. Even those who are recovering, who have survived, overcome such an illness only by enduring a crisis that weakens them almost to exhaustion. It is, therefore, more than ever our unshakable will not to draw back in this battle for our people before the most terrible fate of all times, but rather to obey firmly and loyally the law to maintain our nation. The Almighty created our people. In defending its existence, we defend his work. The fact that defending it brings boundless misery, suffering, and pain makes us love this people even more. It also gives us the hardness necessary to do our duty even during the worst crises, and to do our duty not only to decent, eternal Germany, but also to those few who, lacking honor, have separated themselves from their ethnic community. In this fateful battle, we know but one command: He who fights honorably can save his life and the lives of those he loves, but he who undermines his nation through cowardice or lack of character will die a disgraceful death. National Socialism's greatest accomplishment is that it awakened and hardened this spirit in our German people. When the clash of this great world struggle is replaced by the bells of peace, people will realize what the German people has gained through this spiritual rebirth: nothing less than its very existence in this world.

A few weeks or months ago, Allied statesmen openly said what Germany's fate would be. Several newspapers warned them that they should be more discreet. It would be better to make promises, even if one had no intention of fulfilling them later. As a fervent National Socialist and fighter for my people, I want to make it absolutely clear to these statesmen that any attempt to influence National Socialist Germany with Wilsonian phrases demonstrates a complete ignorance of today's Germany. It is not important that the lie is the close ally of democratic political activity, but rather that each promise that these statesmen make to a people is worthless today, since they are no longer in a position to fulfill any such promises. It is as if a sheep were to promise another sheep that he would protect him from a tiger.

I repeat, therefore, my prophecy that England will not be able to tame Bolshevism, but rather it will increasingly have to develop according to that spreading disease. The democracies will not be able to get rid of the spirits they have summoned from the steppes of Asia. All those smaller European nations that capitulate, trusting in Allied assurances, will face complete extermination. Whether that happens sooner or later is irrelevant—it is inevitable. The Kremlin Jews are motivated only by tactical considerations, which lead them to act brutally and immediately in one case, a little more slowly in another. The end will always be the same.

ADOLF HITLER

Germany will never suffer that fate!

The guarantee of that is the twelve-year battle we fought within our own land. Whatever our opponents do, and however much damage they inflict on German cities, the German landscape, and above all on our people, it pales against the lasting misery and misfortune that would befall us if the plutocratic-Bolshevist conspiracy were to be victorious.

On the twelfth anniversary of our takeover of power, it is therefore necessary that we make our hearts stronger than ever before, that we harden our holy resolve to bear weapons, wherever necessary and under any circumstances, until in the end victory crowns our efforts.

I wish to leave no doubt today about something else. Despite an entirely hostile environment, I chose my own path within Germany. As someone unknown, I pressed on until final success. Often, people said I was finished, and they always wished I were, but in the end I was the victor! My life today is guided just as surely by my duty.

My duty consists solely in this: to work and fight for my people. I can only be released from this duty by him who called me to it. Providence spared me from the bomb that exploded only five feet from me on 20 July. It was intended to wipe me out and end my life's work. I see the Almighty's protection on that day as proof of the duty I have been given. I will, therefore, follow this path in the coming years. Without compromise, I will serve the interests of my people, regardless of all suffering and danger, filled with the holy conviction that, in the end, the Almighty will not forget him who wanted nothing else in his life than to save his people from a fate that they never deserved.

I therefore appeal to the whole German people, and above all to my old fellow fighters and to all our soldiers, that they resist with even greater and harder spirit until—as once before—we can lay the wreath of victory on the graves of those who died in this great struggle, saying to them: And you have won in the end!

I expect that each German will do his duty to the utmost, accepting any sacrifice that is demanded, and must be demanded, of him. I expect that each healthy person will put body and soul into the battle. I expect that the sick, the infirm or those otherwise disabled, will work with their last strength. I expect that those living in our cities will forge weapons for this battle. I expect that farmers will provide as much food as possible for the soldiers and workers in this battle. I expect that all women and girls will support this war with the utmost fanaticism, as they have done until now. I turn with particular confidence to the German youth. Because we are a sworn community, we can stand before the Almighty and ask for his grace and blessing. A people can do no more than that each who is able to fight does fight, each who is able to work does work, and that all together sacrifice, filled with but a single thought: to preserve freedom, national honor, and thus their future.

However great the crisis of the moment may be, we will master it in the end through our unbreakable will, through our willingness to sacrifice, and through our abilities. We will survive this misery. The depths of Asia will not triumph in this struggle, but rather Europe—led by that nation that has protected Europe for fifteen hundred years against the East, and will continue to do so in times to come: our Greater German Reich, the German nation!

NOTES

1. His last major message came on 24 February 1945, the anniversary of the proclamation of the Nazi Party platform in 1920, but it was read over the radio by Hermann Esser, one of Hitler's early followers.

2. The source is the *Völkischer Beobachter*, 31 January 1945.

Acknowledgments

The source of each text is provided in the endnotes. With the exception of Joseph Goebbels's "Total War" speech, the texts come from contemporary printed versions of the speeches that had larger audiences than the often unavailable oral versions. In the case of that speech, a full audio recording survives, which I have used to prepare the written text. The speeches by Goebbels in this volume are printed by permission of Cordula Schacht, administrator of the Goebbels literary estate. All translations are my own.

I thank Martin Medhurst for his indefatigable labors to advance rhetorical scholarship, and two reviewers who provided advice that strengthened the book. My research was supported by Calvin College.

INDEX

9 781603 440158